STORY SERMONS
for
BOYS and GIRLS

STORY SERMONS
for
BOYS and GIRLS

Julius Fischbach

2294

New York • *Nashville*

ABINGDON-COKESBURY PRESS

STORY SERMONS FOR BOYS AND GIRLS

Copyright MCMXLVII by Stone & Pierce

Library of Congress Catalog Card Number: 47-5673

Scripture quotations are from the American Standard Version of the Bible, copyright renewal, 1929,
the International Council of Religious Education.

D
SET UP, PRINTED, AND BOUND BY THE
PARTHENON PRESS, AT NASHVILLE,
TENNESSEE, UNITED STATES OF AMERICA

FOREWORD

TELL US A STORY" IS AN AGELESS REQUEST. CHILDREN and their parents, the young and the old, the rich and the poor, the educated and the ignorant—*people* like their information served in story form. The newspaper reporter covers his account of the occasion with a story; the businessman presents his wares with story accompaniment; the teacher makes his facts live with characters and action; the community leader stimulates the thinking of his fellow citizens with recitals of romance and adventure; the preacher challenges his congregation with parables of life. Everyone listens to stories well told.

The story sermons in these pages were told to boys and girls in the midst of a church family during the morning worship. The subject illustrated in each case, and the scripture text used, were in harmony with the subject and text of the sermon later delivered to the adults. Although it is always true that certain members of the congregation will suggest that the junior sermon had more meaning for them than the minister's major effort, this offering to them is a by-product only, and never a planned service. It does, however, bear witness to the fact that people of all ages listen to stories, whether they are intended for their ears or not. This being true, all who have something of importance to present to others are increasingly seeking to strengthen its appeal by adding flesh and blood to the bare skeleton of the subject matter. One of today's demands, for which

7

there is as yet no adequate supply, is for stories to be told.

The field of the story is the world itself and the entire gamut of life. Every day adds its chapters and every human experience is latent with possibilities. Shakespeare said:

> All the world's a stage,
> And all the men and women merely players.

It could as truly be said: All the world's a storybook and all the men and women merely characters. What people do and say, as well as their dreams and longings, are the warp and woof of material for the storyteller. So let us tell our stories—and act them out—and trust that all of them have happy endings.

J. F.

CONTENTS

9

1

What Is Your Name?

Thy name shall be called no more Jacob, but Israel: for thou hast striven with God and with men, and hast prevailed.
—Gen. 32:28

WHAT IS YOUR NAME? NOW BEFORE YOU ANSWER, let me explain. I am asking a more difficult question than you may think. All of you have at least three names. There is, first of all, your family name—Davis or Schaberg or MacArthur or Eisenhower—and all the members of your family are known by that name. Then there is your given or Christian name. That may be Mary or Sue or Frank. That is the name your mother and father gave you when you were born. But you have still another name, and that is the one I am asking you for. What is *your* name—the name you have given yourself by your actions and habits of life day after day?

Let me illustrate what I mean. I once knew a girl whose father and mother named her Florence but her best friends called her "Sunshine." They called her "Sunshine" because she was so good-natured and cheerful all the time that people always thought of sunshine when they saw her.

Now I knew a boy whose parents had named him Roy but all the boys and girls called him "Piggy." Can you

11

guess why they gave him such a nickname? If you had been in "Piggy's" crowd and had watched him for awhile you would probably have started calling him "Piggy" too. You see, if a friend offered Roy some peanuts, he would put his hand deep down into the sack and bring out such a fistful that very few were left. If you let him take a bite of your apple, he would bite clear to the core. He was always snatching or grabbing something and pushing up front, just like a pig shoving the others aside to get to the trough. So he gave himself that bad name.

Our mothers and fathers usually spend a lot of time thinking about names for a new baby, and they try to pick the nicest name they can find. Sometimes they name a boy for his father or uncle, and a girl for her mother or aunt. Sometimes they choose the name of some famous man or woman whom they admire. They do this because they want their boy or girl to be the very finest sort and they feel that no name is too good.

Then each child, as he grows up, begins to make a name for himself. He may be untidy or grouchy or bad-tempered and give himself a bad name no matter how nice the name his parents gave him, or he may be thoughtful and kindly and industrious and give himself a very fine name indeed. Regardless of how many given names a boy or girl may have (and some have as many as three), each boy and girl acquires his real name, which describes his own character.

In Bible times names usually had a meaning, and you could often tell just what kind of person one was by his name. If such a man became a different kind of person, then his name would be changed to show that he was changed. You remember the story of Jacob. His name meant "to take by the heel." You recall how he took advantage of his brother Esau and cheated him out of his birthright and his blessing. Esau became so angry with him that Jacob had to run away from home, but he continued to take people "by the heel" and cheated his father-in-law Laban. Then, after twenty years of absence, Jacob decided to bring all his family back to his old home, and just before he reached home a strange thing happened. He wrestled all night with an invisible wrestler. As he wrestled he thought of all the wrong things he had done, and in the end he determined to live for God instead of for himself as he had done all these years. Then he learned that his opponent was an angel and he begged for a blessing and got it. He was no longer to be one who takes advantage of others, but one who loves God and serves him. So his name was changed from Jacob, "The Heel Snatcher," to Israel, "Prince of God."

You can probably think of other Bible men whose names were changed. Jesus changed one man's name. It had been Simon. Simon was very undependable. He would blurt out something when he should have been quiet, or he would rush up and do something which often turned out to be the wrong thing to do. But Simon was to be a strong, dependable, faithful disciple of Jesus, so Jesus changed his name to Peter, "Rock."

Paul, the great apostle, was a man with a changed name too. You know his name at first was Saul and he was a persecutor of the Christians. He would search out Christians and put chains on their wrists and take them to prison. He did everything he could to frighten and

13

discourage followers of Christ. Then a great change came over him when he met Christ face to face on the road to Damascus. Forever after that he was Christ's man and became the greatest Christian preacher and leader of all time. So we know him as Paul, the apostle.

Now I want to ask you again, and you may answer it to yourself rather than say it out loud if you wish: What is your *real* name?

2

All Together, Please!

> So *we, who are many, are one*
> *body in Christ, and severally*
> *members one of another.*
> —Rom. 12:5

THERE WAS A TERRIBLE COMMOTION AT THE CORNER
of Capitol and Ionia streets, and it seemed to come from
the big stone church building, and on Sunday morning
too! Yes, it sounded like a church squabble. As the sound
of voices rose louder and louder, each seemed to be trying to drown out all the others and win the argument by
greater noise than the rest. Some claimed that the stones
in the walls were the most valuable and important part
of the whole building because they were not stones cut
from a quarry, but were beautiful, natural, fieldstones,
brought from the farms of various parishioners. They
held many memories of old homesteads, as well as serving to form the walls. Then there was the argument,
insisted upon over and over, that the big stained-glass
window was the real attraction of the building, for
what would a building be if it were all solid wall and
no light could come in? The window was both large and
beautiful, for it was made of colored glass, with many
lovely figures of people and designs, and people always
liked to look at it when they came to church. In fact it
was said—and it must have been true—that one serv-
iceman, coming back to town after two or three years

with the army in the Pacific, came to the church just to look at the window again, and was heard to remark that even on Iwo Jima he had dreamed of that beautiful window and it had been to him a symbol of his religion, helping him keep his faith in that distant part of the world.

There were arguments put forth too about the decorations on the walls and the great beams that support the roof and the pews in which the people sit. Each of these was considered so important that there could not be a church building without it. Take the plaster and the paint, for instance. Some argued that a church with cold stone walls would be an impossible place to worship, except for the covering of plaster and the attractive coating of paint that covered it. Then came the argument for the pews. It was claimed that if it were not for comfortable seats, no one would care to come there to worship at all, since people would not want to stand for an hour at a time. The service was usually longer than an hour for often the preacher forgot himself and preached on and on, far beyond the proper time to close. Talk about standing for that! It was out of the question, for people would really be worn out if there were no pews to sit in.

But the deepest voices that could be heard in the wrangle, and the highest pitched voices, were contending for the foundation of the building and for the roof. "Just think," ran one argument, "what this building would be without a strong, deep foundation. Why, it would all crumble and collapse and be nothing but rubble in no time at all!" "All right," was the high-pitched answer, "what good would all your solid foun-

dation and walls do if there were no roof? Just think
of the rain, the cold in the winter, and the heat in the
summer pouring down, if there were no good old roof
to protect everything."

Then there was the contention that the organ was the
most important part of the church. People could not
worship without music, and it took a big, strong organ
with many pipes and great volume to lead the singing
of the hymns and accompany the choir with their an-
thems. It was more than suggested, time after time, that
people really enjoy the music more than any other part
of the service anyway, and therefore it was the organ
that made the church what it is.

But suddenly all this commotion quieted down and
the church building became so still that you could have
heard a mouse run across the floor, if there had been a
mouse there, which, of course, there was not. You
see, the minister had come down to the church very
early that Sunday morning because he wanted to preach
a great sermon that day and he thought he would practice it a bit before the people came. But he had heard the
noise and the wrangle about what was the most important thing in the church building and, being used to
hearing arguments and sizing them up quickly, he realized that the old building was having a little misunder-
standing within its own many parts. Yes, the walls
thought they were important—most important, in fact
—and so did the windows, the doors, the pews, and all
the other parts of the building.

So the minister forgot his sermon for the time being
and did a little preaching to the old building itself. "You
ought to be ashamed of yourselves," he began, "each

17

one of you talking about his own importance! Of course
walls are important, but so is the roof and so are the
pews and the books in the racks. But don't you realize
that it takes all these parts standing together to make a
church building? Before you proud fieldstones were
built into the wall, you were just rocks that the farmer
piled in the corner of his field to get you out of the
way of his plow. And you plaster, you were just sand and
lime, and you pews, you were just boards piled in a lum-
beryard. You see, building a church has brought all of
you together and made each one of you useful because
you are all part of something big. Now I don't want to
hear any more wrangling and loud talk. Every one of
you settle down and do your part and we will have
a truly beautiful and useful church building here on
this corner of our city. And remember too, even as important as a church building is, it is the *people* that make
the church, and not just the stone, mortar, and paint."

After that everything was quiet indeed for the minister had spoken wisely. But a peculiar thing happened.
The minister laid aside the fine sermon he had prepared
for that morning and looked up in the big pulpit Bible
the place where Paul writes: "So we, who are many, are
one body in Christ, and severally members one of another." He announced as his subject that morning: "One
Body in Christ."

3

Gold and Goats' Hair

> *This is the offering which ye
> shall take of them: gold, and
> silver, and brass, and blue, and
> purple, and scarlet, and fine
> linen, and goats' hair.*
> —Exod. 25:3-4

WHILE THE CHILDREN OF ISRAEL WERE WANDERING
in the wilderness for a period of some forty years, their
church, or meeting place for worship, was called a "Tabernacle." This was a portable church building made in
the form of a large tent. It is not to be thought of in
terms of any tent we might see today, for it was very
ornately and expensively fashioned. It is said that Moses
received the plans for its construction while he talked
with God on Mount Sinai. In order to secure the many
materials needed, an offering was taken and all the people were asked to give what they could. Here are some
of the materials needed: Gold, silver, brass, fine linen
dyed blue, purple, and scarlet, the skins of rams and seals
dyed red, acacia wood, spices for the anointing oil, oil
for burning, precious stones, and *goats' hair.*

It is interesting to read about the building of the
Tabernacle and to learn how all these materials were
used. Gold was used in many places: to overlay and
adorn the altar, the ark of the covenant, the table of
shewbread, etc. The candlesticks were of solid gold.

The linen was made into curtains and formed the inner walls of the meeting place. Acacia wood was used as a framework to support the roof and the walls of the tent, and also for tables and other pieces of furniture. The precious stones were set in gold in the breastplate which the high priest wore when serving before the altar.

To me one of the most interesting articles in the list is goats' hair. What in the world would goats' hair be used for, especially in a fine temple? Actually it was one of the most important materials of all. It was from goats' hair that the canvas cloth for the tent itself was made, and the ropes to hold it up, and the carpets for the floor. The goats' hair tent really made a building which housed all the beautiful furniture and fixtures that were used in the worship services. The fine linen, the precious jewels, and the costly equipment of the Tabernacle would have been exposed to the weather had it not been for the tent of goats' hair that housed it.

Another important thing about goats' hair was the fact that it was so plentiful that everyone could bring at least a bit of it, for every family had a few goats. This meant that every person in the entire nation of the Israelites could have a part in the building of the Tabernacle. No one was left out. In that great and important building project every man, woman, boy, and girl was invited to help. Some of the rich persons brought gold and silver and precious stones. Some of the women, who were skilled weavers, brought fine linen. Some of the men went into the forests and cut down trees and brought the wood that was needed. Certain daring fishermen went to sea and caught the seals or porpoises whose skins were used for the storm roof, stretched over the top of the tent. But I imagine that the goats' hair was brought mainly by the boys and girls who had none of these unusual or costly things to give but did have a goat or two. I imagine those boys and girls were just like boys and girls today. Some of you have a goat, or you have a country cousin who has one. I'm sure you would like to have one to hitch to your wagon and take you for a ride. And I'm sure that if you did have such a goat, and the church needed some goats' hair, you would be eager to clip your goat and bring the hair to the church.

It might seem funny to talk of putting goats' hair on the offering plate in church and it would be most unusual, but thinking about it suggests that boys and girls have a place in the work of the church today, just as they did in the days of the Tabernacle. We do not need goats' hair today for we build our churches of stone, brick, steel, and wood, but boys and girls have things the church needs and which they can bring. We are not even building a church for we already have one, but we need the service of every person in our church family to build the church program and to help build Christ's kingdom in our community and far and wide around the world. As we think of the list of things that are needed, it is even longer than that required for the making of a tent or building. We need money, and all can give some, even if it is a small amount. We need consecrated time, prayer, thoughtfulness, kindness, patience, imagination, and helpfulness one to another. Perhaps we could lump all of these needs together and say we need love in the hearts of each and every one, love prompting each to give and do whatever he has that can

21

be used to the glory of God. We need voices to sing, and hands to greet strangers, tongues to teach and tell the gospel story, and time to make friendly visits with those who are ill. We would never finish our list of services, for each person can think of something he can do which another might not have thought about. God wants and uses all our gifts. Let us never think that because we have no gold we are not welcome or useful. Goats' hair is needed too, and the work could not go on without it. "Gold and goats' hair" is a good phrase to remember, and it is an invitation too: Come and bring what you have and help in the greatest business on earth—God's business of building a happy world.

4

Milkweed Missionaries

Go ye therefore, and make disciples of all the nations.
—Matt. 28:19

THE OTHER DAY AS I WAS DRIVING ALONG A MICHIGAN highway I had an unusual experience. The sun was shining brightly, the day was warm, and a stiff breeze was blowing. All at once the air was filled with a soft white downy something, and at first I thought it was snowing. But it couldn't be snow for the air was warm, and anyway this was only September and no time for snow to be flying.

The "snowstorm" was so heavy, and the air so filled with the downy flakes, that I pulled over to the side of the road to see what it was all about. The big "flakes" seemed to be coming from a field on the right. The "snow" was rising from the ground instead of falling from the sky. Then I saw that it was the "missionary movement" of the milkweed plants. Yes, that is just about what it was, for the field on the right was just a mass of milkweed, and the pods had popped open, and the little downy parachutes that carry the seeds were being blown out of the pods and up into the air as the wind breezed by.

I wondered where the tiny seeds were going in their parachute carriers. As I watched they rose higher and higher and moved off out of sight. If the wind was strong enough, they may have gone many miles before they finally settled down to earth. Some dropped just across the road but others went on and on to other fields far away.

Then I began thinking of the milkweed and its good war record. Perhaps you were one of the thousands of boys and girls who went out into the fields to pick milkweed pods for the use of our servicemen abroad. You see, someone discovered that the soft milkeed "silk" that is found in the pods is so light and buoyant that it makes the best kind of filling for life preserver belts and vests to keep persons afloat when they fall into the water. The material used in these life preservers before the milkweed down was substituted, was called "kapok" or "silk-cotton," and it came from trees in Java, Ceylon, and the Philippines. During the last war, when it was impossible to get kapok from these distant lands, something was needed to take its place and the milkweed served very well.

So we must go back and make another count of the miles the milkweed seeds traveled in their missionary journeys. The wind carried them a few miles and then they settled down and grew into more milkweed plants and enlarged the milkweed "factories" and produced more and more milkweed for life preservers. Then when the boys and girls went out into the fields and collected the pods and sent them to Uncle Sam to use for filling life belts, they started on a much longer missionary journey.

Can you see them stuffed into bags, loaded onto trucks, then packed into bales and put on the train to travel to distant factories where they were needed as fillings for these life belts? But their journey was only begun, for after the lifebelts were finished they were shipped in all directions—to Uncle Sam's air corps men in England, in Africa, in the South Pacific, and all around the world. They were on all the ships that sailed the seven seas. Everywhere around the globe these milkweed missionaries were tucked away for use when men of the Army, Navy, or Marines were adrift on the ocean.

What a splendid job the milkweed plants did! They saved thousands of lives as they kept afloat men and women who had fallen into the sea. The milkweed plants were at work along the coasts of the Americas, the coasts of Europe, all over the Mediterranean Sea, and scattered over the wide stretches of the Pacific Ocean.

Our imaginations are not quite big enough to follow the gift of the milkweed plant in sending out its pods of silk to be used for saving life all over the globe. The milkweed teaches a great missionary lesson. It would take just as great imagination to picture what our missionary gifts do all around the globe, not just in saving the lives of men and women, but in telling the story of the gospel of Christ, so that men, women, and children can know God's love for them and can live happier lives as they give their hearts to him and serve him day by day.

Jesus said: "Go ye therefore, and make disciples of all the nations." Some of you boys and girls one day will go to distant lands as missionaries. Some will be missionaries closer home. But all of us can be missionaries to all the world as we give our money to be used to help send preachers, teachers, and doctors, and to help build churches, schools, and hospitals.

5

I Don't Like Him!

> *Nathanael said unto him, Can
> any good thing come out of
> Nazareth? Philip saith unto
> him, Come and see.*
>
> —John 1:46

TEDDY CAME HOME FROM SCHOOL ONE AFTERNOON
and entered the house with the announcement: "There's
a new boy in school and I don't like him!"

"What is there about him you don't like, Teddy?"
asked his mother.

"I just don't like him," said Teddy, "that's all."

"What is his name and where does he live?" asked
mother.

"I don't know his name and I don't care where he
lives," answered Teddy.

Now Teddy was a bit foolish as well as discourteous,
so mother took him to task and asked a lot more questions. As far as she could tell, the only reason Teddy
did not like the new boy was because the stranger wore
peculiar-looking clothes. So mother called up the teacher to find out something about the new family that
had moved into the neighborhood. She found out that
they had come from a community of Dutch people, who,
since they all lived together in the United States, had
kept many of the customs and practices they were used to
in Holland. Their clothes were peculiar to Americans,

being the roomy, wide skirts and trousers which the Dutch people in Holland like to wear.

I suppose first impressions were what caused Teddy to think that he did not like Joost. You will be interested to know that Teddy and Joost soon became acquainted. They often visited in each other's homes and they became the best of friends. In fact, one day about three months later, Mrs. Johnson was looking for Teddy and a neighbor said: "I don't know exactly where he is, but I'm sure if you find Joost you will find Teddy too, for they are always together."

Teddy, that day in school, jumping at conclusions about Joost just because he did not know him, made the kind of mistake people are making all the time. It has been going on for hundreds of years. If you will recall the New Testament story of Jesus' first disciples, you will remember about Philip and Nathanael. When Philip met Jesus he was so happy that he immediately went to find his friend Nathanael, and said excitedly: "We have found him, of whom Moses in the law, and the phophets, wrote, Jesus of Nazareth, the son of Joseph." [1] Nathanael, jumping at conclusions, just as Teddy did about Joost, said: "Can any good thing come out of Nazareth?"

Nazareth was a small town, not a large city like Jerusalem. It was a town where many newcomers to Palestine lived, and many of the older residents had gotten the idea that it was not the kind of a town where one would want to live. Nathanael had probably gotten that idea from talking with people who had never even been in Nazareth and did not know what they were talk-

[1] John 1:45.

27

ing about. It was just an impression and it was an erroneous one.

Philip was a wise friend. He did not argue with Nathanael but said simply: "Come and see." That was what Nathanael needed to do. He decided that he did not like Jesus even before he saw him or met him. We know that when he did go to see him and got acquainted with him, he loved him and became one of his twelve disciples.

Some years ago our family was traveling through the West and we came to a little town one day that once might have been thought of as a town that did not amount to anything. No one had ever heard of it. It was just a little town in Oklahoma where the climate is dry and hot. Only about three thousand people lived there, and if anyone were going to Oklahoma, he would go to Oklahoma City or Tulsa, not to Claremore. But something good came out of Claremore—Will Rogers, one of the friendliest men our world has seen in many generations. He traveled throughout our country and in many foreign lands and carried good will wherever he went. He was always cracking jokes and telling stories and making people laugh. He was always thinking and talking about the brighter side of life and everyone liked him. He started out as a cowboy but ended by being a good-will statesman.

Will Rogers was killed several years ago in an airplane accident but people have not forgotten him. Recently I heard a man say: "If we only had Will Rogers today, he would do more than anyone else to help our world think in terms of peace and good will." Today, in Claremore, there is a memorial to Will Rogers and thousands of people every year—yes, probably hundreds of thousands—visit that little town just to see the memorial because they think so highly of Will Rogers. Just inside the entrance of this memorial building is a statue of Will Rogers and underneath it these words, which are good for all of us to remember: "I never met a man I didn't like."

Yes, we often do not like people we have never met. If we met them we would discover something likeable about them. We have all heard people say: "I don't like the Japs." The chances are they are not acquainted with a single Japanese. Joseph C. Grew, our former ambassador to Japan, certainly knows the Japanese people well, and he said of them: "For me there are no finer people in the world than the better type of Japanese."

Like Teddy, people talk about the Negroes and the Jews and people from foreign lands, saying: "I don't like them." Like Teddy, they would probably change their tune if they knew some of the people of any of these groups. They would find something good to admire in them and they would make new friends.

Whenever we are tempted to make a blanket statement about anybody or any place, let us remember Nathanael's experience, and then "come and see" as he did.

6

Doing Good

Who went about doing good.
—Acts 10:38

FIVE WORDS IN THE BOOK OF ACTS TELL THE WONDER-ful story of the daily life of the greatest man that ever lived. These words are a sort of thumbnail sketch of Jesus. The words are simply: "Who went about doing good." Just five words about Jesus, but every word is loaded with meaning and action.

Now I have known numbers of men and women—yes, even boys and girls—of whom it could have been said: "They went about doing." I mean that these people were busy, usually going somewhere and usually doing something, but it would not be truthful to say their actions were always good. Often what they did was harmful to someone else. Sometimes they were busy just amusing themselves or doing something to satisfy their own selfishness.

The outstanding trait of Jesus was his unselfishness. He was always helping someone. As we read about his life we find him daily ministering to people in trouble, healing the sick, or comforting the lonely. He never took time to think about himself and his own welfare but was always serving others.

We can close our eyes and imagine Jesus walking along the road with his disciples. His bright, sharp eyes are constantly looking this way and that in search of opportunities to do good. Over there he notices a blind man groping his way, tapping with a cane. Quickly he goes to the blind man's side, speaks a cheering word to him, and heals him of his blindness. What happiness and joy he brings to this man now seeing for the first time in his life! Going down by the Sea of Galilee, Jesus sees crowds of people. They have heard of the great teacher and have come to listen to his words. He teaches them in parables and stories, plainly and simply told, so they can understand. They go home with hope in their hearts because of the message they have heard. On his way home Jesus meets a cripple and a leper and other people in trouble. Although he is tired from a hard day's work, he takes time to minister to each one of them in turn.

Those five words in Acts tell not only about the daily life of Jesus but also give us his idea of the meaning of life itself. He thought of life, with all its powers, as being God-given, and therefore to be used in ways that please God day by day.

There are really only two ways we can live—either for God or for ourselves. If we believe, as Jesus did, that all our talents, our time, our money, and all that we have belong to God, then we will gladly use them all for him and will follow the example of Jesus, "who went about doing good."

Once when a great preacher was to visit a small town to speak to the Christian people there, the man who was to meet him at the station wondered how he would recognize his guest, as he had never met him or seen him before. He was told: "Just look for a tall man helping somebody." Sure enough, when the train came into the station, there was a tall man helping a mother and her little children off the train with their many bags and bundles. So the guest preacher was easily recognized. Like the Master, he was busy "doing good."

We too will reflect the spirit of Jesus as we try every day to find ways to be useful. Certainly there are many opportunities. At home, at school, on the playground, and at church, we can lend a hand and help with jobs that need to be done. We can speak kind words and scatter sunshine with our smiles, and we can even reach a hand of helpfulness across the ocean and help the missionaries preach the gospel and minister to those who are hungry or sick or in great distress. As we give our money to Christ through the church we join hands with thousands and thousands of other Christians of many churches so that together we can reach clear around the world in Christian service.

Isn't it grand to be Christ's helpers and, with him, to go about "doing good?"

7

Bones

*Daniel purposed in his heart
that he would not defile himself with the king's dainties,
nor with the wine which he
drank.* —Dan. 1:8

ARE YOU TICKLISH? BETTER GET SET, THEN, FOR I AM
going to look for some of your bones to see if you have
just the ones you ought to have. First of all, the funnybone. Have you ever heard of it? Perhaps you have felt
it when you bumped your elbow on a table and had
a very peculiar tingling sensation for just about half a
minute. Sometimes this is called the "crazy bone" but
it really is not a bone at all, but a nerve that crosses
over the bone in your arm and cries out for help when
it is mashed against the hard bone. When boys and
girls giggle at everything and find it hard to be serious,
we wonder if they do not have altogether too much
funnybone.

How about your wishbone? Where is that located in
your body? Actually this is not a human bone either,
though I have never seen a boy or girl, or a man or
woman for that matter, who did not act like they had one
somewhere in their system. Perhaps it is located in the
brain or in the imagination. At any rate, all of us like
to wish for things even though while we are doing the
wishing we know it won't do any good at all. When I

was a boy we used to make a wish when we saw the first star in the evening, and as we made our wish we would say:

> Star light, star bright,
>   First star I've seen tonight;
> I wish I could, I wish I might,
>   Have the wish I wish tonight.

We also made a wish if we saw a white horse and there was something that went with that wish too. We would "stamp" the horse by touching our finger to our tongue, then to the center of the palm of our hand, and then strike the palm with our fist. Did you ever do that? But it is still true that wishing doesn't get us anywhere unless we add plenty of hard work to the wishing.

The third bone, which I know all of you have and all of you use, is the jawbone. We have no trouble finding that bone and it gets plenty of exercise. I am not referring mainly to the workout it gets at the table three times a day, but rather to the exercise it gets when we talk. How that jawbone works up and down as we get together and get into discussions and arguments or just get to talking things over! Talking is fine, but hours, weeks, and even months of talking would never build a house. It wouldn't even start to dig the cellar. After talking over the plans, it takes hard work to get the thing done.

Now I come to the most important bone in our bodies —the backbone. It is that backbone that enables us to stand up straight and be a boy or girl, man or woman. It is that backbone that stands for courage, determination, and perseverance, these traits that are so important for the accomplishment of anything worth while. Without the backbone we would crumple up like a rag and be a spineless something like a jellyfish. With backbone we have strength, grit, and drive.

The Bible is filled with stories of strong men and women of God who proved that they had backbone. The one I have in mind is a boy who was taken prisoner to a strange land, but determined to be true to his convictions no matter what happened. I'll tell you something about him and see if you can tell me his name. He was carried away by the Chaldean army to Babylon. There, with three other boys, he was to be fed wine and rich food every day from the king's table, and be schooled and trained for important leadership. This boy and his friends had been taught not to eat certain foods, especially pork, and not to drink wine. He did not outright refuse the king's "dainties," but he suggested to the king's servant in charge of the boys that he try them out for ten days on vegetables and water and then compare them with the other boys who had been fed the rich food and the wine. So it was that at the end of the ten days this boy and his friends proved to be brighter and stronger by eating vegetables and drinking water, and they were allowed to continue their simple diet.

I'm sure by this time you know that the boy I have been talking about was Daniel. Daniel was as fine an example as any I know of uprightness and determination to stand by his high standards and do only what he knew to be right. Perhaps you can remember other stories about Daniel. For instance, the experience he had in the lions' den after he refused to stop praying to God. He was true to God and to himself regardless of the threats made against him. His backbone was certainly sturdy and straight.

So funnybones, wishbones, and jawbones have their places, but we need *backbones* to get important things done and to stand for the right when temptations come. Feel your back up and down right now to be sure that backbone is in its right place. An Irishman once said of boys and girls: "They are the backbone of the community. It is our business to train that backbone and bring it to the *front.*"

We don't want our backbone in front; we want them where they should be, backing up our good intentions and giving us the determination and strength to make real the things we wish for and talk about. So let us brace up our beliefs with backbone, and stand up and work for our ideals.

8

A Blunder That Blessed the World

> *Blessed are your eyes, for they see; and your ears, for they hear.* —Matt. 13:16

EVERYONE WHO HAS EVER LIVED HAS MADE SOME mistakes in his life. Usually he is sorry for those mistakes and often ashamed of them. It is a wise man indeed who can use his errors and blunders to gain understanding and profit by the mistakes he makes.

From some five hundred and forty years back in history comes the story of a clumsy mistake that changed the history of the world because the boy to whom it happened made capital out of a catastrophe.

Here is the story. In the old German town of Mainz there lived a boy by the name of Johannes Gensfleisch. That name may sound peculiar to you because it is German. It would sound funny to you in the English translation for the name means "John Gooseflesh." Now John was like other boys his age and he liked to do things with his hands. He particularly liked to carve wood with a knife and he did a nice, neat job of carving. One day John got the idea he wanted to carve out the letters of his name from tree bark and he set to work. Soon he had all the letters shaped and then he placed them in line in the proper order and they spelled JOHANNES GENSFLEISCH.

Right here I must tell you that John's mother was a dresser of parchments. As you know, in ancient times the skins of sheep, goats, and calves were prepared for use as writing material. The hair was removed from these skins, they were washed and scraped, rubbed down with pumice, and stretched on frames. When the work was carefully done they made excellent paper.

But getting back to our story, John's mother had a pot of purple dye heating over the fire in the fireplace and one or more fine parchments on stretchers lying before the fire to dry. A fireplace is a natural center for everyone doing anything in a room, so John was playing with his bark letters in that same crowded spot. As luck would have it, one of his letters dropped and fell plunk into the pot of purple dye. John grabbed for it before he thought, and rescued it from the pot, dripping with dye. It was hot, of course, and he no sooner had it out of the dye pot than he dropped it right on a fresh new parchment!

You can imagine what happened—at least some of the things that happened. Of course the dropped letter, soaked in dye, ruined the parchment. John's mother was very angry. I imagine there must have been some sharp words and some hurt feelings (besides hurts elsewhere) but I can see John insisting that he be allowed to pick up his letter from the parchment and put it back into the line that spelled his name. When he did pick it up, surprise of surprises! it left an imprint on the parchment, just like the carved letter itself—a capital H!

Inventions do not always pop into an inventor's mind in a flash. Sometimes a peculiar thing that he sees or hears sticks in his mind and he keeps thinking about it and then some day, perhaps years later, he sees new light and a big new idea shapes up. We do not know just what happened in John's case, but it does look like here was a boy who decided to make his blunder work good for him. He kept thinking about that ink spot on the parchment that was the very image of the letter he had carved. At any rate, about thirty years later all Germany was talking about a man by the name of Johannes Gutenberg, who was doing miracles with a machine called a printing press.

Now we need to say a word about that change in John's name. Perhaps John did not like to be called "Gooseflesh" any more than you would, but he had the privilege of changing his name, for it was possible for a boy in Germany to decide to take his mother's name instead of his father's if he chose. This seems to be what John actually did.

We said at the beginning that John's invention changed the history of the world. That is a very strong statement to make, yet it is true that the invention of printing, more than any other mechanical process, has changed every phase of life; for printing means books, magazines, and newspapers, and these mean education and the scattering of news, and the printing press works for every kind of business in the world and helps everything that men do.

It is a wise boy or girl who can make a benefit out of a blunder. Who knows but that some of our blunders are just opportunities that we stub our toes on so we will not walk over them and never see them at all?

9

Lemmings

*Enter ye in by the narrow gate:
for wide is the gate, and broad
is the way, that leadeth to destruction, and many are they
that enter in thereby. For
narrow is the gate, and straitened the way, that leadeth unto
life, and few are they that find
it.*   —Matt. 7:13-14

IN THE MOUNTAINS OF NORWAY AND SWEDEN LIVES A
little animal which once in ten or twenty years does a
thing so unusual that his name has become known all
over the world for this strange action. He is the lemming, a small short-tailed mouse. He is just about five
inches long and is yellowish-brown in color, marked
with darker spots of dark brown and black. He eats
birch roots, mosses, and grass roots. In the winter, when
the snow is deep, he burrows under the snow in all directions searching for food. The fact for which he is
famous—or it might be called infamous—is his great
migration march.

Here is the story. For some reason, which no one
seems to be certain about, the little lemmings get rest-
less and begin leaving the mountains and moving down
into the valleys. Some naturalists and scientists think
the restlessness is caused by lack of food and the lemmings move out to search for more food. At any rate,

a great movement begins and actually millions of lemmings start toward the sea. They move along in parallel columns like a marching army and they march in a straight line. They are very stubborn about this and will turn neither to the right nor to the left. If they come to a haystack they gnaw through it, and only a solid rock will cause them to go around. When they come to a stream they dive right in and swim across. They climb mountains and wade through swamps. They rest and eat during the day and march all night long.

As might be expected, many larger animals prey upon these lemmings. Foxes, lynxes, ermine, and other animals follow them and devour them by the hundreds. Farmers kill them with clubs for they completely ruin any field they travel through. They simply eat up every bit of grain or grass in their pathway. They fall into wells and poison the water. They pollute springs and pools. But so determined are they that nothing stops the migration until they reach the sea. Then they plunge right in and swim out and out until they are exhausted and drown. The lemmings in the rear do not learn from the example of those in the front that have drowned, but the entire army marches on into the ocean until all are drowned.

This is probably the greatest example in all nature of the danger of going with the crowd and doing just as the crowd does. Any lemming could save his life if he did a bit of thinking for himself and decided to turn to the right or left and leave the crowd. But none do. Once started, they keep moving on and on to final destruction.

There is danger in crowds among people as well as

among lemmings. In fact, the state of mind that comes from being part of a crowd is responsible for some of the most terrible things people do. It is called "mob psychology." When such crowds have gathered, men have lynched Negroes and tortured and killed innocent people because the crowd became insane. In a crowd of that kind you will find people who had no thought of harming anyone, and certainly would not have done any violent thing alone. When they became part of the crowd they caught evil ideas and evil passions just as one catches a disease. In the crowd they were not themselves.

The same thing is true of small crowds too. You know there is a saying that "three make a crowd." One boy will work or play by himself and get along splendidly. A friend comes along and the two of them work or play and have a good time. Sometimes, however, when a third comes along and makes a crowd they begin planning and plotting things to do that get all three into mischief. It is usually gangs of boys that get into trouble with the police. The mob spirit takes possession and the boys are not themselves.

In his Sermon on the Mount, Jesus gave some very fine advice in this matter. He said: "Enter ye in by the narrow gate: for wide is the gate, and broad is the way, that leadeth to destruction, and many are they that enter in thereby. For narrow is the gate, and straitened the way, that leadeth unto life, and few are they that find it."

That's the right idea! Open that narrow gate. Let the crowd go its way. Make up your own mind. Don't be a lemming. Be a man!

10

Ash Heaps and Atoms

> *God so loved the world, that he gave his only begotten Son, that whosoever believeth on him should not perish, but have eternal life.* —John 3:16

AMONG THE CHOICE TREASURES IN THE CITY OF Florence, Italy, stands the form of a young man skillfully chiseled from marble and known as one of the world's greatest works of art. It is Michelangelo's "David." Tradition has carried down an interesting and encouraging story about this statue. A marble merchant offered to Bandinelli, a rival of Michelangelo, a block of marble upon which to try his skill. Bandinelli, with a glance at the stone, refused to accept it, saying that it was hopelessly lacking in the requirements necessary to produce good sculpture. Some time later, Michelangelo, strolling through the marble yard, chanced upon this discarded slab. Instantly his inspired eye saw in the crude stone the material he was seeking for a masterpiece. Out of the castoff stone, returned to the marble yard as imperfect, came the creation which marked its creator as the master artist of his day, and perhaps of all time.

Not only have works of art come from castoff and discarded materials, but many of the articles we use today and consider so important that we could not well get along without them, are products of the ash heap and the scrap pile. Recently we have all been greatly excited over the new discoveries about the atom. Our imaginations are not able to picture the amazing new things that will be possible by the use of atomic energy. It will heat our houses, drive our automobiles and trains, and send great ships across the ocean. Men are even planning rocket ships to travel to the moon and other planets. But do you know that one of the important discoveries that led to the understanding of the atom came from an ash heap? You have heard of radium and of Madame Curie who discovered it. This discovery, along with one other made a few years before by Henri Becquerel, changed the whole idea scientists had about matter because it introduced the new fact called "radioactivity."

But let us get back to the ash heap. When Marie Curie started searching for this new substance, she found that it most probably could be located in an ore called "pitch-blende." Now pitchblende is used in making glass and it is a rather expensive ore. Madame Curie was poor and unable to buy this costly ore and for a time she wondered what she could do about it. Then she remembered that after pitchblende had been used in making glass, a large part of the ore was thrown away. It was just an ash heap which no one wanted and was just in the way. She decided that she could work with this discarded ore just as well as with the ore fresh from the mine. So she had some of this ash heap ore hauled to the old shack of a building where she was working and got busy boiling it down. She was not interested in the rough pitchblende, but just in the residue left after many hours of boiling.

Week after week, month after month, year after year, for four long years Madame Curie worked. She literally boiled down tons and tons of the castoff ore from the ash heap of the glass factory. She worked in an old building that leaked when it rained and was cold in the winter and hot in the summer, but she worked on just the same. Then one day the hard work was all done and she put together the many bits of grounds she had gathered and made the final boiling down to see what would be left at the very last. This last tiny bit of grounds proved to be what we now know as the world-famous radium.

Madame Curie became famous and has blessed the whole world with her discovery, which is used to treat cancer and also led to an understanding of the atom.

Just as radium gives aid to the sufferer from cancer, and just as radium was found in an ash heap, so we are reminded of the spirit of Christ, who saw men and women, castoff and worthless in the eyes of other men, and discovered in them something precious to God. They are "diamonds in the rough." They are souls that can be saved and used of God to bless the world. No one anywhere is worthless. All men and women, boys and girls, are children of God. You and I can be discoverers for him and find such discouraged people and tell them of God's love for them. Not matter whether they live in an alley, in a shack, or on the avenue in a fine house, God loves them all and wants them to know his love and share his gift of life more abundant. "God so loved the world, that he gave his only begotten Son, that whosoever believeth on him should not perish, but have eternal life."

11

One Thousand Servants

*I am debtor both to Greeks and
to Barbarians, both to the wise
and to the foolish.*
—Rom. 1:14

OF COURSE MORSE CAN MAKE GOOD GRADES AT
school," said Jerry in defense of his own poor record.
"His dad has plenty of money and there are dozens of
servants around his house to do the work. He doesn't
have to do a thing but study!"

Now there is a question whether Jerry wished for
dozens of servants in his own home so he could spend
all his time studying, but since it was the day before
Thanksgiving, and since it was a good time to show
Jerry how many folks were helping him to live happily, his father said: "Does Morse have only a dozen servants? Then you are much more fortunate than he, for
you have at least a thousand."

"What's that, dad?" said Jerry. "Why we don't have
even one servant, and I wasn't joking about Morse for
I have been in his house and there are servants everywhere; a cook in the kitchen, a maid to clean the house,
a gardner, a chauffeur, and I don't know how many
more."

"I wasn't joking either, Jerry," said his father. "I
haven't counted all your servants recently, but I would
say you have at least a thousand working for you, and
that is a very conservative estimate."

That remark really stirred Jerry's curiosity and he wanted to know who the servants were and why he had not seen any of them if they were working for him. He wanted to know just what they were doing and where they were staying.

"Well," said Jerry's father, "take that breakfast you just ate. Had you thought how many people prepared it for you?"

"Sure, dad, nobody but mother, and of course I am thankful for mother; but in our house she has to do all the work in the kitchen, and all the cleaning and washing."

"Yes," said father, "that is true in a way, and in another way it is not true. Mother has dozens and dozens of helpers you don't always see around the house. For instance, where did that cereal come from, and the cream and the sugar, the cocoa and the cinnamon toast?"

"That's easy," said Jerry. "I brought most of it home from Bailey's grocery yesterday. We had the cocoa and the sugar, but those came from Bailey's too about a month ago."

"But, son, did you ever ask yourself where Mr. Bailey gets all these groceries?"

"Sure, I know the answer to that one too, dad," said Jerry. "He gets almost all his groceries from Redman Brothers, the wholesalers."

"I don't want to be too inquisitive," replied dad, "but where do you imagine Mr. Redman found all those different groceries and articles of all sorts for our table?"

"Oh, I begin to get your point now, dad! You are thinking of the farmers who raised the corn, the people

47

in the factory who made it into flakes and boxed it, the truckmen who hauled it to the train, the trainmen who brought it to our city, and all the dozens of men and women who had something to do all along the line until it reached the grocery store."

"That's exactly what I had in mind," said dad. "And what you said about the corn flakes is true of the sugar, the cocoa, the cinnamon, and every other item we use. Furthermore, that great crowd of servants lives all over the world. If you think just a moment about the sugar and cinnamon and cocoa—and these are just a few of the items we get from abroad—you will realize that people in India and South America and Africa and China, in fact, in every country on earth, are working for us every day and helping to make life happy for us here in our little home."

"I guess I hadn't thought of it quite that way, either," said mother. "I do get pretty tired sometimes, but I think it would be a good thing for me to remember how many people all around the globe I have working for me and helping me."

"Yes, it is certainly true of all of us, whether we are at the office, at school, in the kitchen, or even on the street. All the time and everywhere we are being served by thousands of people we never see and will never meet."

So it happened that next day at the Thanksgiving dinner, instead of reading the thanksgiving psalm he usually read on that occasion, father turned to Romans and read: "I am debtor both to Greeks and to Barbarians, both to the wise and to the foolish."

12

Thanks for Yesterday

I thank God, whom I serve
from my forefathers in a pure
conscience.   —II Tim. 1:3

Our forefathers in the United States were wise in setting aside a special day to be given over to thoughtfulness about the many blessings we enjoy and thankfulness to God for his goodness to us. We call it Thanksgiving Day. Of course we ought to be thankful everyday, and every hour of the day for that matter, but Thanksgiving Day helps us "get our pitch" with the hope that we will stay in tune and be thankful all year long.

Usually when we begin counting our blessings and naming them one by one, we look around us and think of the things we can see right at hand. There are so many other blessings which begin far away beyond our sight that it would be a fine thing if we would think of them too and be thankful for them. They are the foundations of most of the things we have today. If the foundation had not been laid, there would have been no building for us to enjoy now.

A hundred-year-old story comes to us from Williams College in Williamstown, Massachusetts. Mark Hopkins was president of Williams College, and he was a man who became well known throughout the United States because he understood his students so well and was such a fine teacher. It was once said that Dr. Hopkins on one end of a log and a student on the other made a college. It did not take buildings and a campus but just a great teacher and an eager student.

But not all Dr. Hopkins' students were eager or dependable. One of the other type, a boy from a rich man's family who thought he could buy his way anywhere, was sent to Dr. Hopkins' office one morning, charged with defacing property by carving his name on a desk. The young man was not ashamed or sorry. He strutted around and asked Dr. Hopkins to tell him how much damage was done and he would pay the full amount. He pulled out his pocketbook with a flourish and assumed a very arrogant air.

Dr. Hopkins' answer to this fellow is well worth quoting: "Young man," he said, "put up your pocketbook. Tomorrow at prayers you will make public acknowledgment of your offense or you will be expelled."

Then, in explaining how serious the young man's offense was, Dr. Hopkins said: "Rich young men come here and take that tone as if they could pay for what they get here. No student can pay for what he gets in Williams College. Can any student pay for the sacrifice of Colonel Williams and our other benefactors? For the heroic sacrifice of half-paid professors who have given their lives that young men might have at the smallest cost a liberal education? Every man here is a *charity* student."

What Dr. Hopkins said of his students at Williams College is true of all of us everywhere we are. All of us in a sense are "charity cases," because all of us are using every day what was given us by men and women who lived and worked and sacrificed years ago to make the beginnings that have developed into the institutions and organizations we have today. For instance, take your school. You have a fine school building and a fine school system, yet not one of you boys and girls has paid a cent on either the building or the salaries of the teachers. Your fathers pay taxes to support the school, but even they did not help with the foundation work, for the town was here before they came, and the school system was already started.

What is true of the school is true of the church too. In the eleventh chapter of Hebrews we have a long list of people who were pioneers and lived by faith. They were foundation builders and, as the writer says, none of them lived long enough to enjoy the benefits of the things they worked so hard to build, but their children and grandchildren and others after them received the blessings. The church you attend has a long, long history. It may not be very old itself, but still it has a long history, for in some way or other it came down from that first little group of disciples who met in an upper room in Jerusalem, to pray and seek God's will and try to be true followers of Christ. The gospel story was passed on from father to son, down, down through the centuries. When churches were established the members were eager to share their knowledge of Christ and his gospel with others who had no church, so evangels and missionaries were set out, some to places near at hand and others to distant lands.

Our own church is a good example. Ninety-five years ago fourteen Christian people who had come to the little village of Lansing from cities in the East, decided to organize a Baptist church. This church, then, was a gift to Lansing from many Christian churches further east who had trained the fourteen men and women who organized it. As First Church grew and became stronger and larger it too thought in terms of others who were not favored with a church in their neighborhood. So it sent deacons to start a Sunday school in the southern part of the city. This later came to be South Baptist Church. Then other deacons were sent to the north-eastern part of the city and their efforts resulted in the organization of the Pennsylvania Avenue Baptist Church. Three other such churches were also established: Olivet, on East Michigan Avenue, Judson Memorial, on South Cedar Street, and Valley Farms Baptist Church, on route twenty-seven, north of the city. During this same time the mission field was not forgotten, and financial aid was given to help establish and support churches, schools, and hospitals in many lands around the world.

Every church and every Christian should be expressing gratitude in terms of service. We cannot thank the people who built our foundations for they are probably dead, but we can say "thank you" in a better way—by passing on to others some of the good things we have received. We can do for them what others have done for us. That is making Thanksgiving Day a happy day and one that stretches out over the whole year and other years to come.

13

What Are You Worth?

*How much then is a man of
more value than a sheep!*
—Matt. 12:12

Businessmen often ask: "what is he worth?"
They mean, how much money and property, stocks
and bonds, does the man have? If all his material possessions were sold, what would the price be in dollars
and cents?

Boys and girls would not be worth much on that
basis, for few of the boys and girls I know have very
much money or very much property either. Here is a
boy who has a fine bicycle and here is a girl who has a
half-dozen nice dolls and a good pair of skates, but all
of these things, if sold, would not bring a great deal of
money.

Again, boys and girls would not be worth much if we
considered just their bodies. Someone has figured out
the chemicals in the average person's body: the calcium,
iron, phosphorus, and so forth, and he says that if all
these substances that are found in the human body were
distilled and packaged and sold, the total would not be
worth much over ninety-eight cents. Our bodies—considered only as a combination of chemicals—would not
be worth very much, and a boy or a girl would not
be worth so much as a man or a woman.

Our bodies are not worth a great deal when used as

machines to pull and haul and lift and shove. We can carry burdens, it is true, and do many useful things, and boys and girls, as well as men and women, are needed for work of many sorts. Yet a horse or an elephant is much more useful and a machine, such as a tractor, can work hard all day and not get tired. So our bodies, as work-machines, are not of great value.

How about our worth as sources of knowledge and useful facts? I once heard of a mother who was approached by a book salesman who wanted her to buy an encyclopedia set. She said she did not need one because her daughter was being graduated from college and would be home in a very few days! I am sure that mother meant her remark as a compliment to her daughter, as she thought her very smart, yet we all know that we forget almost as fast as we learn, and one little *World Almanac* contains more facts than would be found in the minds of all the members of all the college graduation classes in the country. So we are not worth much as sources of information.

If we really are going to find out what a boy or a girl is worth, the best place to inquire is not at the bank or the stock market but at the home of that boy or girl. Did you ever think how high a value your father and mother put on you? They must think you are worth a lot for they spend hundreds of dollars every year for your food, your clothing, and all the things you need and use day after day. But even this does not prove the value they place on you. I heard of a man and his wife who had more money than they knew what to do with but still were unhappy because they had no child. They knew a father and mother who had several children and they particularly liked the youngest boy of that family. He was a very lovely child and they had fallen in love with him. In fact, everyone who knew him loved him. He was such a fine little fellow. This rich man thought he could buy anything with his money, so he decided to go to that mother and buy her youngest son. He was ready to offer a million dollars cash. Do you think he came back home with the boy? Of course not. No true mother or father could ever put a price on a son or a daughter: All the money in the world would not be enough to buy their child.

I think the best way to answer the question: "What are you worth?" is to think of the words of Jesus when he talked about the worth of persons. He called attention to the birds, reminding us that God takes care of them every day, and then he said: "Are not ye of much more value than they?" [1] He talked about a sheep falling into a pit and the farmer rushing out and working hard to save its life, and again he asked the question: "How much then is a man of more value than a sheep!" But the most beautiful story of all is the one Jesus told of a shepherd who had one hundred sheep and at night, when he brought them in to the fold, found ninety-nine in the flock, but one was missing. So he put the ninety-nine in the fold and and went out into the night looking until he found the little lamb that was lost. Then he said that God is like that. He loves each child so much that he is grieved when even the least of them is lost, hurt, or in distress.[2]

So just as a child's worth is best determined by the love of his father and mother, so the worth of all of us is

[1] Matt. 6:26.   [2] Matt. 18:12-14.

55

measured by God's love, and he loved each and all of us so much that he sent Jesus to live and to die for us that we might live forever.

When we think of it that way—since God makes our worth so great by his own love for us—we ought to live our best for his sake!

14

The Increasing Christ

> *He must increase, but I must decrease.* —John 3:30

ONE DAY WHEN JOHN THE BAPTIST WAS TALKING with his disciples they told him about the crowds that were going to see and hear Jesus, and they were a bit jealous for their own teacher. Then John, whose real purpose was to be a "forerunner" or announcer of Jesus, said to them: "He must increase, but I must decrease."

That was a noble and unselfish thing for John to say and it was a prophecy too, for from that day to this the cause of Christ has increased and multiplied. Take the first disciples Jesus called. Jesus invited Andrew to come with him and Andrew was so delighted that he immediately told his brother Simon (whom Jesus later renamed "Peter"), and Simon became Jesus' follower too. The very next day Jesus found Philip and said to him: "Follow me." Philip gladly followed him, and he was so happy that he told his friend Nathanael, and Nathanael also followed Jesus.

So it was that those who met Jesus told others and the crowd grew larger and larger. There was always a great crowd when Jesus preached and it increased as the days went by. We are told that on the day when Jesus told his disciples good-by, and departed from them to go to his heavenly Father, there were more than five hundred of those who were known as Jesus' followers. These were not just the ones that liked to hear him preach but the ones who loved him and wanted to do his will.

Then the day of Pentecost came and Peter preached the sermon. It was a great day, for the Spirit of God was there and people heard the gospel gladly. It was a great international service too, for there were people there that day from many nations and many parts of the earth. The most important result of the service was that three thousand people gave their hearts to Christ and became his followers. That was a wonderful increase for our Christ.

Down through the years, from that day to this, Christ has been increasing. I took down the *World Almanac* the other day just to see how many Christians there are now. This is what I found. In the United States alone there are more than fifty-one million Christians. In the whole world there are nearly six hundred million. I know those figures are so large we cannot begin to realize what they mean, but we can see that Christ's kingdom is spreading over the whole globe. There are Christian missionaries preaching to all races and nations and there are Christians in every land in the world.

But the most wonderful part of all is that you and I can help Christ increase by our own work in winning others for him. Perhaps I can best illustrate that by the life of one boy who became the world's greatest evangelist. His name was Dwight. He was born in East Northfield, Massachusetts. When he was seventeen years of age he wanted to go to work, and since he had an uncle in the shoe business in Boston, he decided to go to Boston and try to get a job there. His uncle

Samuel was very glad to give him a job, but he required five things of him: (1) Dwight must sleep in the big room over the store, where other clerks lived in a sort of dormitory. (2) He must stay off the streets at night and always be in the dormitory at an early hour. (3) He must never go to a questionable place of amusement. (4) He must take his meals at the home of Deacon Levi Bowers. (5) He must attend Mount Vernon Church every Sunday.

Dwight agreed to do all this, which, of course, his uncle meant for his own good. About a year later his Sunday-school teacher, Mr. Kimball, came down to the store and put his hand on Dwight's shoulder and said: "Dwight, don't you feel it is time for you to give your heart to Jesus?" Dwight did, and he later referred to that call of his teacher as one of the high spots of his life.

The next year Dwight went to Chicago and there he became interested in the boys and girls who were wandering about the streets on Sunday and he gathered them into a Sunday-school class. This class soon became so popular that it had to move to a large hall. It was not long before the teacher began preaching as well as teaching and this young man's fame spread and spread as he got invitations from other cities to preach in them. Dwight L. Moody—for that was his full name, and a name all of you know—became one of the greatest evangelists of all time. He preached all over North America and also in England, where he held revival meetings, and thousands of people came to hear him. He held one meeting in Chicago at the same time as the World's Fair, and during those nights more people went to hear him preach than went to the fair. His crowds numbered as many as sixty and seventy thousand. But the finest part of it was that people not only came to hear him but they gave their hearts to Christ. It was estimated by some of his friends that during his lifetime Dwight L. Moody won a million souls for Christ! What a multitude of people! What an increase for Christ!

You and I can never hope to be as great an evangelist as Dwight L. Moody, and we will probably never preach such a sermon as Peter preached at Pentecost. But we can do as Andrew and Philip did, and each of us can tell our brother or our sister or our friend about Christ and win them for him. Yes, all of us can have our part in the great increase of Christ, and there is nothing we can possibly do that will make us happier than to tell others about our Lord and help them to know him.

15

World Without Christmas

*Glory to God in the highest,
and on earth peace among men
in whom he is well pleased.*
—Luke 2:14

JANEBETH AWAKENED WITH A TERRIBLE THOUGHT
in her mind on Christmas Eve. She had had a bad dream.
It was a nightmare, I suppose. She called out to her
mother: "Mother, isn't Christmas really coming this
year?"

"Why, of course, dear," said her mother reassuringly.
"This will be the happiest Christmas of all. The war is
over and so many of the boys will be back with their
families. Yes, it will be a glorious Christmas—and today
is Christmas Eve."

"But what if it didn't come? What if it never had
come at all!" said Janebeth.

"What in the world is the matter with you, child?"
said her mother. "What have you been dreaming anyway?"

Then Janebeth told about her horrible dream. Everything seemed to be darkness. There was no happy music,
no beautiful lights, and no joyous laughter. There was
nothing but gloom and despair.

So it was that at the breakfast table that little family group began talking about Janebeth's dream, and
from that dark picture turned to the joyous thought of

Christmas and the happiness it brings. What a contrast it was, and the bright picture was the real one, the other only a nightmare that would soon be forgotten.

"Since we know that Christmas has come, and will come every year, and it means so much to everyone the whole world over," said father, "why not try to imagine what the world would be like if Janebeth's dream were true, and Christmas did not come. Just what would our town be like? What would be left out that we have now?"

"We wouldn't have any Christmas carols or Christmas music," said Janebeth, for even then they were listening to beautiful carols coming over the radio.

"That's right," said her mother, "and we wouldn't have had the beautiful Christmas pageant you children gave at the church last Sunday night, nor the singing of the 'Messiah' by the choir."

"No candy socks and pep'mint canes," contributed five-year-old Bob.

"Yes, and no vacation for the schoolchildren and no hard work for the businessmen," added dad.

A world without Christmas! What would need to be taken away from our town and our world if there had never been a first Christmas? Christmas is the birthday of Christ and with his coming came Christianity, and with the coming of Christianity came a whole new idea of life and its meaning. Without Christmas and Christ we would not have the Christian church and the Sunday school. Think what our towns and cities would be like if all the Christian churches were gone! Our schools would have to go too. It was the church of Christ which sponsored the first schools in this country. These first schools were started in order that churches might have trained ministers. Then more schools were started for boys and girls in order that, as Christians and members of the churches, they might be able to read and understand the Bible.

Our libraries, hospitals, Y.M.C.A.'s and Y.W.C.A.'s would be missing too, and all those organizations and institutions which conduct character-building programs. There would probably be no community chest either, for it is the thoughtfulness and concern of Christian people that suggests such things. Practically every good thing in our community would be lacking, for the spirit of unselfishness and service is inspired by Christ and is a characteristic of his true followers.

At Christmas time there is joy everywhere. You feel it as you go shopping. It is reflected in the gay windows of the stores and in the happy greetings of the people as they meet on the street. There is music in the air and everyone seems to be in good humor.

The story of Jesus' birth that first Christmas day tells of the angels singing and saying: "Glory to God in the highest, and on earth peace among men in whom he is well pleased." In John's account he talks of Jesus as the "light of men." [1] Music and light, carols and candles, are part of Christmas and they greatly help in making Christmas the happiest time of the year. With the music and the light goes the generous heart and the desire to give gifts to others, just as the wise men gave gifts to Christ.

The spirit of Christmas is the spirit we need every day in the year.

[1] John 1:4.

16

Trimming the Christmas Tree

She brought forth her firstborn son; and she wrapped him in swaddling clothes, and laid him in a manger, because there was no room for them in the inn.
—Luke 2:7

YES, YOU HAVE GUESSED IT! THIS MORNING WE ARE going to trim a Christmas tree. We are going to trim it so it will tell the story of Christmas. Sometimes those who trim the tree put on everything they can find that looks bright or even gaudy, but we want our tree to represent the true Christmas spirit, so we must be very careful what we hang on its branches.

Of course you are going to help me. I want all of you to come right up here and pick out just the right objects to use, and then you put them on the tree where you think they ought to be. Now wouldn't it be fun to tell the story of Christmas, and then see if we can find things here on the table that we can put on the tree so that the trimmed tree itself will be not just a Christmas tree but a *Christmas story tree*?

The story began on a hillside. "And there were shepherds in the same country abiding in the field, and keeping watch by night over their flock." [1] Then an amazing thing happened. It must have startled those

[1] Luke 2:8.

sleepy shepherds; perhaps it frightened them too, for suddenly an angel appeared and a bright light shone in the sky, and the angel spoke a message of good tidings and great joy to all people: "For there is born to you this day in the city of David a Saviour, who is Christ the Lord." And then, as you recall, a host or choir of angels appeared and sang a wonderful anthem: "Glory to God in the highest, and on earth peace among men in whom he is well pleased." Then as the angels dimmed out from sight and the music faded away in the distance, the shepherds excitedly rushed away to see this child whom the angels had announced to them.

What shall we use to picture that story on our tree? A lamb? Yes, that is part of the story, and a shepherd's crook too. Anything else? Certainly John, an angel. Will you please hang it on the tree? We will need plenty of light too and I have already strung lights all over our tree and we will turn them on later, for every part of the Christmas story is filled with light and beauty.

As we continue our Christmas story, we see some men in the distance riding from the East. They look like very important persons and they are dressed in robes like kings. "Now when Jesus was born in Bethlehem of Judea in the days of Herod the king, behold, Wisemen from the east came to Jerusalem, saying, Where is he that is born King of the Jews? for we saw his star in the east, and are come to worship him." [2]

They inquired of Herod, the king, and he was greatly troubled. He thought this new king would take his throne and he was determined to get rid of him at once.

[2] Matt. 2:1-2.

So he called the chief priests and scribes and asked them about the prophecies that told of Jesus' coming and where he would be born. They answered that the Christ would be born in Bethlehem of Judea. Then Herod sent the wise men to Bethlehem to search for the Christ child and charged them that when they had found the child to come back and tell him all about it so he too could go there and worship the new king. We know that these wise men did not return for they were told that Herod wanted to kill the child, and they went home by another route.

When the wise men came to Bethlehem and found the Christ child they fell down and worshiped him, and "opening their treasures they offered unto him gifts, gold and frankincense and myrrh." [3]

What shall we put on the tree to tell this beautiful story? A star? Fine! Where do you think the star should be? Right at the very top of the tree? That is just where we shall put it and put a light in it too, the brightest light of all so it will shine out as it did that first Christmas night to guide the wise men from the East. What else shall we use? Camels? Good! Now you will find some little urns and bottles there on the table. They are to represent the frankincense and the myrrh, and the tiny bag represents the gold. If you will tie them on the tree we will see if all the trimmings are on. Is anything missing? Cows and donkeys? You are right, Michael. We'll ask you to place one cow on the tree and Sarah can place a donkey to remind us that Jesus was born in a stable.

Now who wants to turn on the lights? We cannot all

[3] Matt. 2:11.

turn them on. I will give that honor to the youngest one of the group. Nancy may turn on the lights. Ah! Isn't it beautiful and bright? It is glowing with light, just as Christmas should be, and as you look at the branches, with the many interesting objects hanging from them, you are reminded of the Christmas story itself. So we will call this our "Christmas Story Tree."

Now all of us will circle the tree and hold hands and sing a Christmas hymn. What would you like to sing? "Joy to the World"? That is just the one to finish our Christmas story:

> Joy to the world! the Lord is come;
>   Let earth receive her King;
> Let every heart prepare Him room,
>   And heaven and nature sing.

17

Holy Night

*There was the true light, even
the light which lighteth every
man, coming into the world.*
—John 1:9

THE BIRTH OF CHRIST HAS INSPIRED MANY ARTISTS TO
paint a masterpiece. Such pictures date far back through
the centuries. They also date from recent months and
years, for artists are still painting pictures depicting the
birth of the Christ child. These artists are of many nations and races, and all of them have a wonderful story
to tell through their pictures. The picture we are going
to study was painted over four hundred years ago by
the Italian artist Antonio da Correggio, and is called
"Holy Night." It is one of the great pictures of all time
and today shares the honors with Raphael's "Sistine
Madonna" in the Zwinger Gallery in Dresden.

Correggio's masterpiece might have been called "Light
of the World," for the Christ child, at the center of the
picture, radiates a soft light which lights the face of
his mother, who bends over him adoringly, and the faces
of all the figures in the composition. It is the light from
the child's face that lightens the whole stable.

Several early callers have come in to see the child,
but the mother is so charmed by the lovely face of her
baby that she does not seem to recognize their presence. These visitors are two shepherds, an older man

and a younger one, and a woman with a market basket. The older shepherd, by the waving gesture of his arms, seems to be telling the mother of Jesus about the amazing sight they have just seen on the hillside, when the angels appeared to them. The younger shepherd is looking up into the older man's face, as though living all over again that wonderful experience. He is holding by the collar a big dog, which, dog-like, is eager to jump up and put his paws on the crib and lick the face of the baby Jesus.

The visiting woman must have been on her way to or from the market, and, seeing the unusual light and hearing the excitement of other visitors, dropped in to greet the new baby. By her expression and gesture she shows her delight and joy.

In the background Joseph can be seen having quite a bit of trouble handling a donkey. This may have been the donkey which Mary rode on her trip to Bethlehem, or it may be a donkey that was quartered in the stable and which is rather unruly because he resents the use of his feed crib for a cradle. At any rate it is an interesting detail that attracts our attention. The stable itself is an unusual one, for we see a huge stone column right in the middle of it, and we wonder why a stable should be so magnificently built. Perhaps the answer is that this stable is a make-shift affair, and is located in the ruins of what was once a stately building.

There are several other figures in the upper left-hand corner of the picture. These are angels, and perhaps they are supposed to be part of the angelic choir that greeted the shepherds. These figures were painted by the artist probably to suggest that heaven itself was interested in the birth of Christ, and the angels came to visit the manger birthplace of the king.

This picture, as is true of all great pictures, is too large in its story and idea to be contained within its frame. It suggests an outreach far beyond the picture itself. This is shown by the dawning light in the background, where we see the distant hill and the village, and the idea comes to us that this Christ child, who is the Light of the World, is brighter than the morning light itself. Even as the day is dawning, so a new world is coming with Christ as its leader and Lord.

If you and I were to try to add something to such a beautiful picture, we would not attempt to add that touch with a brush and paint but we could add a song and a prayer. I am sure that if we stood in the art gallery and gazed upon the picture itself, with its lovely colors and soft light, we would thank God for his goodness in the gift of his Son, and say to ourselves that most beautiful scripture verse of all: "For God so loved the world, that he gave his only begotten Son, that whosoever believeth on him should not perish, but have eternal life." [1] There would be a song in our hearts too, a song of rejoicing and of praise, for somehow we need music to express what we feel very deeply.

O come, let us adore Him,
O come, let us adore Him,
O Come, let us adore Him,
Christ, the Lord!

[1] John 3:16.

18

Look Behind You!

> They even carried out the sick
> into the streets, and laid them
> on beds and couches, that, as
> Peter came by, at the least his
> shadow might overshadow some
> one of them.   —Acts 5:15

WHEN THE SUN SHINES THERE IS ONE THING ALL OF
us have, no matter whether we be short or tall, slender
or fat, old or young. Furthermore this something goes
right along with us. We could not forget and leave it
at home if we wished. We cannot fold it up and put it
in our pocket. It goes where we go and it stops where
we stop. Sometimes it tags along behind us, sometimes it
walks beside us, and sometimes it runs along in front of
us. Have you guessed? Yes, it is our shadow!

There is a German story about a man who had no shadow. He looked like other men. He talked and walked
like other men, and on a day when the sun was not
shining brightly he seemed to be just like other men.
But when the sun shone down people noticed something
startling about him. He had no shadow! They stared at
him and wondered. They were afraid of him too.
Wouldn't you be afraid of a man who walked about
in the sun and did not cast a shadow?

But of course that German story was a fairy tale, for
no such person ever lived anywhere. In some parts of

the world, though, people are afraid of shadows. Doesn't that sound funny, for a person to be afraid of a shadow? We sometimes say a timid person would be afraid of his own shadow, but these people I have in mind are afraid of the shadows of other people.

You see, in some Oriental countries people are divided into different classes or castes. They do not know democracy as we do. Poor people are in a low caste and educated people and rich people are in higher castes. The people in high castes have nothing to do with the people in low castes. They will not even speak to them. If a low-caste person touches a high-caste person, the high-caste person thinks he has been injured or made unclean. They have this same idea about the shadow of another person. If the shadow of a low-caste person should fall upon a bowl of rice which a high-caste person is eating, the high-caste person would be afraid to eat any more of that rice for he considers it unclean.

We may laugh at the idea of a shadow hurting anyone or making anything dirty, but it is true that a shadow may do good. The shadow of a friend may give shade to one who is weary and resting, with no protection from the heat of the sun. The shadow of a generous person bending down to help a poor beggar on the roadside would also be a shadow of good omen.

The Bible speaks of shadows and they are always good shadows too. For instance, it says the good man shall "abide under the shadow of the Almighty." [1] In another place it suggests that a good man's presence is like the "shadow of a great rock in a weary land." [2] In the book of Acts there is a word about shadows that shows the

[1] Ps. 91:1.   [2] Isa. 32:2.

72

kindness and the helpfulness of the Apostle Peter. People knew how good he was and also how busy he was doing good. There were so many people who needed help, and so little time to help them all, that friends and relatives of sick people would carry them out by the side of the street where Peter was to pass by so his shadow might fall on them. Peter's shadow was a blessing wherever he went.

Shadows remind us of an important something else all of us have—influence. No matter how small or how large, how old or how young, all of us have influence and cast that shadow on others. You influence your younger brother or sister, your playmates, and even your father and mother. You influence other people too. For instance, you may be so careless in running across lots and damaging lawns and shrubbery that you influence your neighbors to think all children are a nuisance. Then again you may influence them just the opposite way by the thoughtful things you do and say. You may be so helpful about the house and so good-humored that your mother's life is made happy all day long.

Think of the boys and girls you play with at home or at school. Do their mothers groan when they see you coming, or do they feel glad because they do not worry about broken windows and blackened eyes when you are around?

So look behind you! That doesn't mean to keep watching your shadow all the time, but it does mean remembering that you cast a shadow of influence every day, whether the sun shines or not. Be sure your shadow, like Peter's, is a blessing wherever it falls.

73

19

Happy New Year!

*Jesus advanced in wisdom and
stature, and in favor with God
and men.* —Luke 2:52

FOR DAYS AND DAYS THE POSTMAN HAD BEEN BRING-
ing bundles of cards to the door, most of them with large
letters and bright colors saying "Happy New Year." It
was fun to open the envelopes and look at these cards
with their gay pictures, but at the same time it was very
puzzling to Johnny who began to wonder how in the
world a happy new year could come into his front door
on a greeting card.

He was thinking about this on New Year's Eve as
he climbed wearily upstairs to his room. All at once he
heard a tiny little voice calling to him and he realized,
to his surprise, that it was the angel at the very top of
the Christmas tree. As he looked toward the tree the
angel smiled at him and said teasingly, "Why Johnny,
don't you know what 'Happy New Year' means?"

Johnny forgot his surprise at hearing the angel speak,
and said, "Why no, that is what I have been wondering about all day long."

"Well then, I'll tell you," said the angel. "It means
growing taller in your body, wiser in your mind, and
better in your heart."

As Johnny began to think just what that could
mean he remembered a text his Sunday-school teacher

had taught the class just two weeks before: "Jesus advanced in wisdom and stature, and in favor with God and men." The teacher had explained to them that this meant that Jesus grew stronger in his body, wiser in his understanding, and his love for God and his fellow man grew too.

Pretty soon Johnny awakened, for really he must have been asleep when he heard the Christmas tree angel speak, and said to himself: "I know what I'll do. I'll surprise mother and dad by cleaning the snow off the walk before they get out of bed."

That evening, as they were seated around the fireplace, father said to Johnny: "Do you remember that last year we made a mark on the wall to show how tall you were? Come over here and let's see if you have grown any during the year."

Of course Johnny jumped to his feet and stood by the wall as father measured. Certainly he had grown! The mark was two whole inches below the top of Johnny's head. Something inside Johnny seemed to say: " 'Happy New Year' means growing taller in your body."

As they sat quietly watching the fire, mother suddenly remembered that tomorrow Johnny must start back to school, and she also remembered that he must take back his signed report card. She had not seen the card since vacation started and she was afraid it had been lost. Johnny smiled, for he knew where it was, and, in fact, he was very proud of it. Mother was glad too when she looked at it and she said: "Why Johnny, these are the best marks you have made during the entire school year!"

Again something seemed to speak, and it said: "Growing wiser in your mind."

Before mother could sign the card, the telephone rang and father, being closest to it, picked up the receiver. It was Mrs. Brown, a widow who lived next door, and as she talked, father said: "Well, is that so, Mrs. Brown? I'm glad you told me for naturally we want our boy to be thoughtful and helpful as a good neighbor should be." Then he said, "Good-by," and hung up the receiver and said, as though he were making a speech over the radio: "Friends, may I announce that we have with us tonight none other than the good Samaritan in person!"

Then he explained that Mrs. Brown was very thankful to Johnny, who had not only shoveled the snow from his own walk, but had gone right on and shoveled her walk too. Johnny was just a little embarrassed at this and looked out toward the other room, and who should he see but the Christmas tree angel winking at him. Then he understood exactly what "Happy New Year" means —Growing taller in your body, wiser in your mind, and better in your heart.

How Old Are You?

> *Let no man despise thy youth;*
> *but be thou an ensample to*
> *them that believe, in word, in*
> *manner of life, in love, in faith,*
> *in purity.* —I Tim. 4:12

I WANT TO ASK YOU A QUESTION WHICH MAY SEEM very easy to answer, but I warn you that it is much harder than you think. I want to ask you the difficult question: How old are you? John says "ten," Mary says "eleven," and Susan says "eight going on nine." But I say all of you are wrong. You are much older than that.

Who was the oldest man who ever lived? Does anyone remember? Perhaps you almost remember but cannot quite get that long name. It was Methuselah, and the book of Genesis says he lived to be nine hundred and sixty-nine years of age. I know that people say time was not counted in those days as it is now, and they did not figure as many days in the week or as many weeks in the month, and so their years were far shorter than ours. But even at that, I insist that all of us are older than we say or think we are.

Let me try to prove my point. When did Columbus discover America? All of you say in 1492. When was Jesus born? All agree it was about two thousand years ago. Now what I want to ask you is this: If you are only nine or ten years old, how can you tell me about something that happened four hundred and fifty years ago, and even know about something that happened two thousand years ago?

In school you study arithmetic. No one knows actually how old the subject of arithmetic is. The Egyptians had systems of numbers and even complicated forms of mathematics, perhaps two thousand years before the coming of Christ. The Chinese, the Hindus, the Babylonians, and the Greeks, all used mathematics so many centuries ago that we have no record of the time when they did not know how to work such problems. So when you learn arithmetic you add to your mental store knowledge that reaches back four thousand years and more. Yes, it reaches clear back to primitive man, for even those people of the Stone Age learned to count small sums. They probably counted on their fingers—as some of you do now. Since they did not wear shoes, they probably counted on their toes too. It has been said that the reason we count by fives and tens now is because we have five fingers on one hand and five toes on one foot, and ten fingers on both hands and ten toes on both feet. When we use our fingers or toes to count, we are probably acting like the very earliest people, when they counted thousands of years before history began to be written.

You study science in school too. Although we call science modern and think of it as very recent, it too has a long history. Science, as we study it today, is very different from the early forms of science, but perhaps we would never have had modern science if the crude, primitive ideas had not come along first. It is thought that men first began to think in the direction of science when they started wondering about the sun and the moon and the stars. Astronomy was probably the oldest of the sciences. The earliest science that is recorded is the astronomy of the Greeks, about six hundred years before the birth of Christ. But those men of the Stone Age must have thought about the sun and moon too, and wondered what held them up in the sky and made them move across the heavens. They also tried to explain thunder and lightning, and snow and rain, and when they asked questions about these things they were beginning to become scientific. So as you study any kind of science your mind is connecting up with ideas that go away back to the very beginnings of man's life on earth.

These two illustrations are enough for our contention about your age. Though your body may be just ten years old, your mind is of such a nature that it can grasp knowledge that stretches it out over thousands and thousands of years, and gathers up all the facts that men have been able to discover and to learn over all those years of time. We won't argue as to whether a person's mind can be older than his body, but this discussion may help us to understand a little better the advice which Paul gave to his young friend Timothy. These are his words: "Let no man despise thy youth."

It seems as though Paul is saying to Timothy: "Do not be timid or hesitant. You are older than you seem to be, and are abler than you think. Have confidence in yourself and do your best, and you will find you will accomplish what you set out to do."

I think you might well take that same advice. You too are much older than you think you are. You have

79

the finest opportunity any boys or girls ever had in all history. Everything that has been discovered and proved to be worth knowing, you can learn about and use. You do not need to make the mistakes others have made, for you can profit by their errors and do better. You have a mind that can gather up all the facts you need to know, and you can be four thousand years old in knowledge and understanding. Now take Paul's advice seriously. Be confident that you are old enough to be useful, and to play an important part in helping with things that need to be done at home, at school, at church, and wherever you are. "Let no man despise thy youth" but get busy and prove your worth!

Mortimer Muskrat

*Let us not be weary in well-
doing: for in due season we shall
reap, if we faint not.*
—Gal. 6:9

MORTIMER MUSKRAT CAME TO TOWN AND, BELIEVE
it or not, he came to our church! Yes, some boys and
girls on their way to school found him curled up in a
nest of leaves down in a window well. Of course we rescued him from the well and gave him a cordial welcome.

Now I do not know just why Mortimer came to
town. I do know murkrats are very curious, and I presume that since his pond in the country was frozen
over and there was nothing much going on, he just decided to take a little trip to the city to look around. He
may have been looking for some carrots or apples, or even
a banana or two. He probably did not know anything
about the scarcity of food or he never would have ven-
tured into the city, but Mortimer is just a muskrat and
did not know.

You would be interested in seeing Mortimer's home.
Perhaps you have seen it many times and did not know
what it was. Those piles of rubbish you see sticking
up from ponds as you drive through the country are
the homes of muskrats. They make them out of reeds,
sticks, twigs, and grass, and plaster them up tight with
mud. They look pretty rough on the outside but on the

inside there are rooms like a real house. Were you to punch a stick through one of those houses when you are skating on the pond, you would hear some strange sounds if you listened closely. First there would be a rustling and scurrying around inside; then you would hear a "plunk, plunk, plunk, plunk, plunk." Those plunks would be papa and mama muskrat and the three children jumping from their house into the cold water beneath the ice. You would not see them at all for they would swim away under the ice and come up for air at a hole away off at a distance. They do not mind cold water at all. In fact, every night they come out of their warm houses and swim around looking for roots or shell fish, or perhaps some tree bark for supper.

Muskrats are very, very busy folk. They are always either swimming around hunting food, which they bring back to their home or to a special place on the bank, or they are busy building their house. In the summer they leave the big house in the middle of the pond and burrow into the bank and there they raise their babies.

We think of the muskrat as being a small cousin of the beaver. The expression "busy as a beaver" applies to the muskrat too. We might call him "Mortimer, the mechanic," for he is like a mechanic or engineer when he builds his mud house, and always as industrious as can be as he hustles around for materials and food.

But I haven't told you what Mortimer looks like. He is a pretty fellow, with his chestnut-brown fur coat. He is about the size of a big fox squirrel and about the same color, though somewhat darker. His hair is long too. His head is large and his ears small, and he does not seem to have any neck at all. He looks like a great big giant mouse. You know how big a mouse's head is. Mortimer's tail is like a black snake and he uses it like a propeller when he swims, and he can certainly cut the water when he wants to go places.

Muskrats are hunted and trapped for their fine fur. Many of the fur coats we see are muskrat coats. When it is made up into such coats it is called "Hudson Beaver" and looks very much like a real beaver coat. Boys in the country like to trap muskrats and make spending money by selling their hides. Since muskrats are so plentiful and are found in so many parts of the country there must be quite a number of junior muskrat trappers.

Since Mortimer Muskrat came to church I think we ought to give him a scripture text, and I think I know just the one that suits him best. When Paul wrote to the Galatians, he urged them: "Let us not be weary in well-doing: for in due season we shall reap, if we faint not." We can go Mortimer one better. He is just *doing* and very busy with his doing, but we can be busy with our *well-doing*.

22

Behold! Consider!

Behold the birds of the heaven,
. . . consider the lilies of the
field.   —Matt. 6:26-28

NOW DON'T FORGET TO WEAR YOUR RUBBERS, AND BE
sure to button your coat up around your neck, and
keep your gloves on!"

Did you ever hear such parting words? Of course you
have, and you probably hear them every cold day when
you start for school or play out of doors. Did you ever
wish your rubbers were part of your feet and you had
a fur coat growing right on your back like a bear so you
would not need to be always remembering what you
ought to wear and what you must put on?

In the frozen north country there is a backwoods
cousin of Peter Rabbit who never loses his shoes and
never forgets his mittens. Mother Nature has put them
on him securely for all winter and there is no danger
of their coming off until spring.

Have you heard of the snowshoe rabbit? He is an interesting fellow to know. He is much larger than the
bunny or cottontail rabbit we know so well. He is about
the size of the big jack rabbit of the western plains. But
his feet are larger than those of either of his cousins.
You see, as winter comes on the snowshoe rabbit's feet
fan out with heavy fur until his foot is more like a
broad snowshoe than an ordinary rabbit's foot. His

toes are not close together but spread out wide. These broad snowshoe-feet enable the northern rabbit to run very rapidly over the soft snow without sinking down in the drifts. He just skurries over the surface and in this way saves his life from enemies that are after him. Foxes, lynxes, dogs, weasels, hawks, and owls all prey on the rabbit, but he is fast on his feet and when his pursuers bog down in the snow, he flies away like a white ghost.

Even more important for his protection than his big feet is the coloring of this northern rabbit. Again nature takes care of him. In the summer, when the ground is brown, the rabbit is brown also. As the fall weather comes on and the cold wind blows, the rabbit sheds his soft brown hair and a new coat grows. This new winter coat is pure white, just like the snow itself in color. By the time the first hard snow comes Br'er Rabbit has his heavy white overcoat on, and when he squats down on the snow it is almost impossible to see him. This is protective coloring at its best.

There are a number of animals that change their fur from summer to winter colors. This happens to most of them that live all winter so far north that the snow covers the ground for at least half the year. Fitting an animal or bird with special equipment, like the snow-shoe-feet, is also a regular service of Mother Nature for her children. Ducks have webbed feet, as do all birds that frequent the water. Feathers of water birds are waterproofed so that the water runs off instead of soaking in. Climbing animals have claws to grip the bark of trees. Eyes of hunting animals are focused ahead for keen, straight vision. The eyes of hunted animals cover a wide range of vision. They see what is going on at the right and left as well as straight ahead and can catch sight of an enemy sneaking up toward them.

All of these facts are interesting but they are much more than that. They are instructive for us too. They show us some of God's handiwork in the world and suggest material for some very serious thinking on our part. Jesus was always helping his disciples to use their eyes to really see and their minds to really understand. He pointed to the birds flying overhead and said: "Behold the birds of the heaven, that they sow not, neither do they reap, nor gather into barns; and your heavenly Father feedeth them. Are not ye of much more value than they?" Then he called their attention to the wild flowers and said: "Consider the lilies of the field, how they grow; they toil not, neither do they spin: yet I say unto you, that even Solomon in all his glory was not arrayed like one of these."

Yes, even a snowshoe rabbit can teach us the lesson of God's loving care and protection. A rabbit cannot say "thank you" for God's goodness, but we can express our thanks both for ourselves and for Br'er Rabbit too!

23

In Remembrance

This do in remembrance of me. —I Cor. 11:24

TODAY IS COMMUNION SUNDAY. YOU BOYS AND GIRLS will be wanting to ask questions, but of course you would not whisper in church. Since I know there will be questions in your minds, I thought we might answer some of them now, and then you will understand the service and will be very quiet and thoughtful as the bread and wine are being passed.

Notice the words on our Communion table. What do they say? I see you are having a bit of trouble reading them and some of you are squinting your eyes. The letters are what we call "Old English." They are fancy letters with many extra flourishes, and you need to study them a bit to read them. Let us read slowly together:

This Do in Remembrance of Me

So the Communion is a remembering service. It is given to us to help us remember. But who is the "me" to be remembered? Christ, of course. The Communion service is in memory and in honor of Christ.

How do you usually remember important things? Do you just say them over and over until they stick in your mind, or do you use some object to help you remember? When I was a boy my mother often would send me to the store for groceries. She knew I would probably meet other boys on the way and stop to play, so she tied a string on my finger to cause me to remember. When I felt that string and looked at it, I would remember I had an errand to run. I must admit that the string method was not so good, however, for sometimes I would have to go back home and ask my mother what it was she wanted me to remember!

There is a teacher in our church who has something by which he remembers his class. For many years this teacher has taught a class of men. These men think a lot of their teacher, and the other night they had a banquet in his honor and gave him something by which to remember them. Can you guess what it was? A string? No, it was a very costly present. A book? No, but that would have been nice. A fountain pen? I'm sure he would have appreciated a pen, but the present they gave was a gold watch. On the back of the watch they had their teacher's name engraved and then the name of the class and the date. That teacher will certainly remember his class if he lives to be a hundred, for he will be looking at his watch many times a day to see the time, and every time he looks at the watch he will remember the thoughtfulness and love of the class that gave it to him.

We had a big wedding in this church last night. Two of our young people were united in marriage. An important part of the ceremony was the giving and receiving of rings. The young man placed a ring on the young woman's finger and said: "With this ring I thee wed, and to thee I will be true so long as we both shall live."

The young bride then placed a ring on the young man's finger and repeated the same vow. This couple gave these rings "in remembrance." As long as they live, day after day as they glance at these rings, they will remember that beautiful ceremony in the church, the many friends gathered to wish them well, the young men and the young women who formed the wedding party, and the solemn wedding vows. Wedding rings are symbols that carry the memory of the wedding and its deep meaning for the husband and the wife.

Jesus left us symbols by which to remember him too. There in the upper room, the last night he was with his disciples, he did what may have seemed a strange thing to them, though it soon came to be a blessed act of remembrance. He took a piece of bread from the plate on the table, bowed his head in prayer thanking God for his many blessings, and then broke the bread so there would be one piece for each disciple, and said: "This is my body, which is for you: this do in remembrance of me." [1] Jesus placed a piece of the bread to his lips, and the disciples did the same. Jesus had given the bread to them as a symbol of himself—his own flesh. Then he took the cruse of wine that was near the center of the table and poured some into a cup, saying: "This cup is the new covenant in my blood: this do, as often as ye drink it, in remembrance of me." [2] Taking a sip of the wine, he passed the cup around for each to drink a bit.

The disciples did not understand the meaning of this first Communion service that night in the upper room, but they understood it a few days later when Jesus suffered and died for them and for us all. After his resur-

[1] I Cor. 11:24.   [2] I Cor. 11:25.

rection, he himself explained it so all of them understood. After that, each time these disciples came together for worship they took bread and wine, saying again the words Jesus had said to them, and, as they took the bread and wine, they remembered him and his great love and sacrifice for them.

Bread is like flesh in color: it may be white or brown or black. Wine is red like blood. And so we think of these two symbols which Jesus gave us as perfect symbols because they suggest what they stand for. I think the main reason Jesus used them as symbols is because there is never a meal when we do not have bread in some form, and, in Oriental countries, there was never a meal when there was not some sour wine, which was the drink in those day. So Jesus gave as symbols these artilces of food and drink which everyone would see on the table three times a day, and thereby be led to remember him every time they came to the table for a meal, as well as when they had the Communion service in the church.

The Communion service is a time for quiet thoughtfulness and prayer, a time to think of Christ's sacrifice for us, a time to think of our own lives and to pray God to help us be just the sort of person he wishes us to me. *"This do in remembrance of me."*

24

Our Praying Presidents

Lord, teach us to pray.
—Luke 11:1

ONE DAY A DISCIPLE OF JESUS CAME TO HIM AND SAID: "Lord, teach us to pray." Now Jesus' disciples must have known how to say prayers, and they probably had the habit of praying in that sense every day. But they came to realize that to Jesus prayer was more than merely saying words to God. I think they must have known that somehow Jesus' prayers were responsible for his victorious living and his great power for good.

Prayer is the secret of all great living for it is by prayer that we talk with God, learn his will for us, and gain from him the wisdom, courage, and strength we need day by day.

A splendid example in the habit of prayer is given us by the two presidents whose birthdays we celebrate this month of February: Washington and Lincoln. Both were praying presidents, both gave many public testimonies of their faith in God, both urged the citizens of our nation to pray that our republic might continue to be blessed by the Almighty. Abraham Lincoln, in a statement which he made at the time he left his home town of Springfield to go to Washington, united himself with George Washington in his sense of need before God. Said he: "Without the help of God, who ever attended Washington, I cannot succeed. With that help I cannot fail."

There is a story of a prayer incident in the life of each of these great men which has been preserved for us in bronze. The one about Washington is a story told by an old ironmaster who lived near Valley Forge. This old ironmaster was also a Quaker preacher. He told of strolling through the creek at Valley Forge and finding Washington's horse tied to a sapling. A little further on he saw General Washington kneeling on the ground in prayer. He was praying for his troops who were starving and dying of cold during that terrible winter. This picture of Washington is done in a bronze plaque and hangs in the Subtreasury Building in New York.

The bronze statue of Lincoln praying was made by the sculptor Herbert Spencer Houck and is in the Cathedral of SS. Peter and Paul in Washington, D.C. The sculptor was inspired to make this statue by the stories his grandfather told him of seeing Lincoln praying on the battlefield of Gettysburg, in a field made sacred by the blood of the soldiers who died there. We know that Lincoln was accustomed to pray for wisdom when important decisions had to be made, and he himself said that often the burdens of responsibility in the White House "force me to my knees."

The church pews in which these two great Americans worshiped and knelt in prayer are marked with bronze tablets and are visited by thousands of our citizens every week. The pew in which Washington often knelt is in Christ Church, Alexandria, Virginia. The pew in which Lincoln often knelt is in the New York Avenue Presbyterian Church in Washington, D. C. Both of these men are said to have been fairly regular in their attendance at church.

These references have been mostly to the public prayer life of our great presidents at least public enough to come to someone's attention. We know that the background of such prayer must have been the habit of private, secret prayer at home, and Jesus said this is the most important kind of prayer. He said: "But thou, when thou prayest, enter into thine inner chamber, and having shut thy door, pray to thy Father who is in secret, and thy Father who seeth in secret shall recompense thee." [1]

It has been said, and I think truthfully, that "no skeptic has ever sat in the White House." In other words, all our presidents have been God-fearing men. We trust that this will always be so. We want all our presidents to be praying presidents. Let us remember, however, that both president and people must pray, for no president, no matter how great or good, can do enough praying for the whole nation. Let us follow the example of Washington and Lincoln and cultivate the habit of prayer both at home and in the church. "Lord, teach us to pray."

[1] Matt. 6:6.

25

Follow Me!

> *Jesus saith unto him, Follow
> me.* —John 1:43

THERE ARE NO HAPPIER PICTURES ANYWHERE THAN those which artists have painted of Jesus and the children. Some artists have tried to paint the scene as it might have looked on that day in Palestine, when Jesus took a little child and set him upon his knee and said: "Suffer the little children, and forbid them not, to come unto me: for to such belongeth the kingdom of heaven." [1]

Other artists have wanted to be sure boys and girls of today understand that Jesus loves them too, and wants them to follow him in our modern day, so they picture the children, not as Oriental boys and girls of Jesus' time, dressed in bright robes and wearing sandals, but as boys and girls like yourselves, dressed as boys and girls dress today.

This second type of picture has been painted by the artist Tom Curr, and it is loved by boys and girls everywhere because it is a picture that includes boys and girls from everywhere. It is entitled "Follow Me." As we look at it, let us notice how many different races or nations are represented by the children. Jesus is holding by the hand a little Hindu or Indian boy. To the left of the Indian boy is a curly-haired American girl wearing

[1] Matt. 19:14.

jumpers. Then to the right of the little boy, and just behind Jesus, are two boys and two girls. The first girl is from Hawaii or one of the south Pacific islands. She wears a grass dress and has a flower in her hair. Her skin is brown. Just behind her is a little black boy from Africa, and beyond him is a boy whose yellowish features and close-fitting cap indicate that he comes either from China or Japan. The tiny one just coming into the picture is a pretty little miss from Holland. How many other children can you count? Of course you cannot really see them, but the artist painted his picture in such a way that our imaginations do not stop at the edge of the picture, but we think of a whole crowd of boys and girls following Jesus out beyond, with only six of them just coming into view. Certainly this is a true conception, for no one could ever count all the boys and girls all over the world who love Jesus and would follow him wherever he leads them.

But the important figure is Jesus himself. What a kindly face he has. I suppose no artist could ever really paint Jesus as handsome and winsome as he was, but Tom Curr has made his face of Christ very attractive indeed. Although the children are modern children and dressed as children of the different races and nations dress today, Jesus is dressed in the robe of Palestine. His hair is hanging in long tresses and he has sandals on his feet. The artist has added a modern touch, however, and one that expresses action and power. He shows Jesus with his sleeves rolled up as men are accustomed to do when they work or play. The arms of Jesus are muscular too and he is an athletic person, able to romp with the children all day and not tire.

Did you notice the distant city? It is not a city of Palestine, but an American or European city. It is a city with smokestacks and factories. It is a city of business and industry. Jesus and the children are walking down a road that leads to that city, and our imaginations must be busy to fill in the story of the day. Perhaps Jesus met them in the city and took them out into the fields to spend the day. Perhaps they knew he was coming to the city that day and went out early to meet him and welcome him on the road. Perhaps he invited them to meet him this day on the outskirts of the city, and now that the day is drawing to a close and they have had a wonderful time together, he is seeing that they all get safely home.

Yes, there are so many things we can imagine about a picture like this. And with all our imagining and all our thinking we could not possibly include all the truth and all the possibilities of a day in company with Jesus.

The finest part of it is that the picture is a living one. It is not just a wish or a dream. It is real because Jesus is real, and he loves you today just as much as he ever loved boys and girls, and you can love him today just as they did yesterday. Jesus is calling the children today too, and I believe he needs them and asks them to help him to do some of the important things he wants done today. One of those things, and the one which this picture emphasizes, boys and girls can do even better than grown men and women. That is teaching friendship among the races and nations all around the globe. Boys and girls are the same wherever you find them, and even though some of them have brown skins and some yellow or black, all of them like to play, and all of them like to be friends and work and play together. That is just what Jesus wants. He wants to build a kingdom on earth and in his kingdom all people are brothers and sisters regardless of race or color.

Now I want you to look at that picture again, and we will walk right up close and then you will see that we are part of that crowd of boys and girls who follow Jesus. We are the ones who are just beyond the frame. The six who are painted on the canvas are in front and have slipped into the frame, but we are right behind and following Jesus too. Close your eyes for a moment and see if you can still see the picture of Jesus and the children. Then open your eyes again and remember that even though you cannot see the picture as you go home or go to school tomorrow, Jesus is your teacher and your friend. He loves you and says to you too: "Follow me."

26

The Christ of Every Race

*And I, if I be lifted up from
the earth, will draw all men
unto myself.* —John 12:32

THE LITTLE GIRL WHO LIVED IN INDIA WAS DELIGHTED
as she heard stories of Jesus. Week after week, as she
came to the mission school, she heard more stories and
her love for him grew. Then one day the teacher said:
"The pictures we have been looking for have come and
tomorrow I will show you the pictures of Jesus. There
are some which show his boyhood and others the man
Jesus as he went about healing, teaching, and preaching."

Little Mumtaz could hardly wait until tomorrow. She
was very excited indeed and woke up several times during the night thinking it was time to get up and go to
the mission station. It seemed that morning would never
come, but finally the sun shone in her window and she
literally popped out of bed, for she had overslept, and
she hurried to get ready to go to school.

Mumtaz' teacher was a wise teacher and knew how
to keep the best for the last. This meant that many memory verses must be said and many stories retold before
the pictures were displayed. Finally the great moment
came and the picture of Jesus, as a boy of twelve, standing in the temple talking with the learned scribes and
teachers, was unrolled. With a sigh of joy the pupils
gazed at the beautiful picture. But Mumtaz looked in

surprise and then burst into tears. For her the picture was a terrible disappointment. She sobbed and sobbed.

The teacher came to her desk and said: "Mumtaz, what in the world is the matter? Aren't you pleased with the beautiful picture of Jesus?"

"He isn't like I thought he would be," sobbed Mumtaz, "he's *white*."

Here was a little brown girl of India who loved Jesus and, of course, had thought of him as being brown like herself and her father and mother and all the rest of the people in her neighborhood whom she knew and loved.

But do you know that the missionary teacher might have shown Mumtaz a picture of Jesus painted as a *brown* Indian boy? Do you know that pictures of Jesus have been painted by artists of almost every nation and each artist paints his Lord as one of his own countrymen?

Yes, the German artist paints Jesus with the features of a German, the Chinese artist paints him as a Chinese, and the African artist paints him as a Negro. If you go to the library and ask for copies of the pictures which the great artists of all nations have painted of Jesus, you will find that each artist has thought of Jesus as a man of his own race. And this is one of the greatest compliments that men could give to Jesus. Men of all races, when they come to know him, have loved him so much that they have adopted him into their own nation and race and think of him as being one of their own people.

This was suggested by Jesus one day when some Greeks came to meet him and the disciples were not sure Jesus would care to talk with foreigners. When they told him the Greeks were waiting to see him, he said: "I, if I be lifted up from the earth, will draw all men unto myself." Jesus was referring to his crucifixion. He meant that after he was lifted up from the earth on a cross, and had suffered and died for the whole world of men, they would be drawn to him and love him when they understood what he had done for them. That is exactly what has happened. Missionaries of the gospel are in every nation on the globe, and wherever they tell about Christ, men and women, boys and girls, come to know and to love him, and always they think of him as one of their own kind.

One day when Jesus' mother and his brothers were looking for him and he was very busy preaching to the people, he said: "Who is my mother and my brethren?" [1] Then he answered his own question by saying: "Whosoever shall do the will of God, the same is my brother, and sister, and mother."

Little Mumtaz was right. Jesus is Indian and African and Chinese and Dutch and German and American. He is the Christ of every nation and every race, and the day of peace and brotherhood around the world will come when people of all races become brothers and sisters of Jesus because they love him and do the will of God, our heavenly Father.

[1] Mark 3:33.

27

Shadows

> *We know that to them that love God all things work together for good, even to them that are called according to his purpose.* —Rom. 8:28

Do you like to draw pictures? then may i ask another question: How do you begin your picture? If you were drawing a dog, would you start with his nose, his ears, his back, or his tail? Would you entirely finish one part before starting the rest, or would you outline the whole dog and then work on the details?

These may seem to be foolish questions, but I have found that people who like to draw and paint go at it in different ways. The most unusual artist I have talked with is one who begins by drawing the space *around* the object instead of the object itself. What I mean is this: If he were drawing a cocker spaniel, he would study the shape of the spaces above the dog, below the dog, and to the right and the left. Very carefully he would outline these spaces and then the outline of the dog would be in the middle. It would be something like cutting out the picture of a dog and then pasting the pieces that were left over on another piece of paper. The vacant space in the middle would be the shape of the dog.

Do you know that pictures are right-handed and left-handed, just like the people who draw or paint them?

It is possible for a left-handed man to paint a right-handed picture, but if he paints without giving special thought to the matter, he will paint just as he is, left-handed. The same is true of a right-handed person.

But I started out to tell you about shadows and I haven't said one word about them yet. We have been talking about pictures, though, and shadows are the most important part of any picture. In fact if you take a piece of plain white paper, there is always a picture on it—many of them—but no one can see the picture until the artist sketches in the shadows and then it is plainly seen. Years ago when I was studying in an artist's studio, I was trying hard to sketch a picture of a Roman statue. It was not the whole figure, just the head and shoulders which I wished to draw. But even this was proving a very difficult job for me. I had tried and tried, and I was just about to give up when my teacher came up and looked over my shoulder. After watching me for awhile, he said: "You are thinking the wrong way about your picture. You are looking at the high lights and the detailed parts that are so hard to draw. Think about the *shadows*. Study them and draw them, and then you will find it much easier."

So I sat back in my chair and tried to think differently about the picture. That really is what it meant, for I had been thinking backward by trying to draw the bright spots when I should have been seeing and drawing the dark spots, for it is the dark spots that bring out the form and the general shape of any object. As I studied the sculptured head, I saw many interesting shadows. One looked just like a bob white quail. Another looked like the map of Michigan. I began sketching these dark spots and filling them in with my charcoal pencil. Then when I thought I had drawn all the shadows and darkened the outlines, I sat back again to look at my picture and, believe it or not, the whole picture was before me and needed only a few marks here and there to finish it. You see, after all it is the shadows that make the picture, and if they are drawn accurately and put in their proper places, the picture comes out of itself.

Well, I learned two lessons that day: one about drawing and one about life. People have always talked about the shadows of life. If the joys and happy surprises are the sunshine and the bright spots of our daily living, then the sorrows and disappointments must be the shadows. We often feel like complaining when things do not turn out the way we planned them and we are disappointed, or when we work hard and are still a failure instead of a success, we are terribly discouraged. An artist would know that all these shadows are important for a picture. There must be hardships and even suffering if life is to be beautiful. It is these shadows that bring out our character and our true personality, and engrave the picture of our lives where it can be seen by all.

So it is very important that we should use these shadows for our good, and not make the mistake of becoming angry or discouraged when they come. The Apostle Paul gives us a text to think about when he says: "We know that to them that love God all things work together for good, even to them that are called according to his purpose." Now we know that Paul had some terrible experiences. He was stoned and shipwrecked and spent many years in a dark dungeon. He knew what shadows are. But still he says they all work for our good.

Yes, Paul is right. It takes both sorrow and joy, both failure and success, both shadow and sunshine, to make life strong and beautiful. The big thing to remember is that first part of the text: "To them that love God." It is God who makes the difference. It is when we allow God to be our teacher and look over our shoulder and instruct us that we become true artists, not only with our hands but with our hearts as well.

28

Faith on a Raft

> *They that wait for Jehovah shall renew their strength; they shall mount up with wings as eagles; they shall run, and not be weary; they shall walk, and not faint.*　—Isa. 40:31

As I HEARD THE THRILLING STORY TOLD BY LIEU-tenant James C. Whittaker, our guest speaker at the annual banquet of the Y.M.C.A., I seemed to hear over and over again the words of the prophet Isaiah who said long ago: "They that wait for Jehovah shall renew their strength; they shall mount up with wings as eagles; they shall run, and not be weary; they shall walk, and not faint."

Now as you well know, Lieutenant Whittaker was not flying at the time, neither was he running or walking. He, with Captain Eddie Rickenbacker and six others, was floating in a tiny rubber raft on the great Pacific Ocean. There they were, eight men in three frail boats, lost and helpless. For twenty-one days they floated in waters churned continually by sharks and rolled high by waves.

When their plane was forced down because of faulty navigation instruments, they barely had time to get the rafts into the water and get into them. When they got away from the plane and took stock of their possessions, they found their entire food supply was four "anemic" oranges. They were not even healthy fruit but dried and shriveled from having been kept too long. How carefully they divided those oranges! Each was cut into eight pieces and each man had one tiny piece a day for four days!

When the oranges were gone they had no food at all. There were plenty of fish swimming around the boats and one of the men had some fish hooks, but there was no bait and the fish did not care to bite the bare hooks. These men were so desperate that they debated with one another for a long time what part of their bodies they would cut for bait! One said the lobe of the ear would not be missed and would make good bait. Another said a piece out of a toe would be better as it would not be so noticeable a disfigurement. As the debate went on, an unusual thing happened. A sea swallow alighted right on Captain Rickenbacker's hat. Imagine how cautiously, yet how excitedly, the captain must have lifted his hand to grab that bird. He got the bird all right and it was immediately killed and cut up into bait and the fishing was good. The trouble was with the sharks. The small fish would bite fast enough, but unless the men were quick in jerking the fish into the boat, a shark would grab the fish and swallow fish, hook, line, and all. A few fish were landed, however, and cut into equal parts so every man had a few bites of raw fish. Lieutenant Whittaker says those bites were delicious, for starving men are not particular about their menu or how the food is served.

Water was the next problem and there was no water. Then one day it rained. The men soaked up the rain water with their shirts and then wrung out the water into their mouths and squirted it into Mae West life belts to keep for later use. That was a very unsanitary method of storing water, but it did the business and that is what counted with them.

One man of that little group had a New Testament and he had formed the good habit of reading it. The rest wanted to hear it read too. So each evening they drew the three rafts into a circle and read a section of scripture and said the Lord's prayer together. Sometimes they prayed other prayers but none of them knew much about praying. They all learned to pray, however, and God heard their prayers and answered them. That is why those men are alive today.

Lieutenant Whittaker confesses that he was very skeptical at first, for he was not a religious man and did not have any faith in prayer and had not thought much about God. He listened to the others. He saw prayers answered. He felt the strengthening influence of their little evening prayer meetings. Then the final experience came which convinced him of God's presence and help.

It was the twenty-first day of that terrible nightmare on the ocean. The three little rubber rafts had been allowed to float apart hoping they might the better be discovered and rescued. As morning light came, Lieutenant Whittaker and the other two men with him saw before them a long line of palm trees. They were close to land! Being the strongest man of the three, though terribly weak himself, he rowed as steadily as he could for hours and hours. One of the other men relieved him for short spells and the other, being the weakest of the three, helped by pouring water on his back to counteract the scorching heat of the sun.

They were just about to reach the land when a gust of wind and a strong current of water swept them out to sea. They were discouraged, for they were all exhausted and felt that they could not row any longer. But again they gave their best and approached the land when another gust of wind swept them even farther out to sea.

This was the end of the rope for all of them. They felt that all hope was lost now—all hope unless God took a hand in their rescue. Lieutenant Whittaker prayed. He simply told the Lord they had done their best and there was nothing more they could do without his help. Then it was that help and strength came. Then it was that Isaiah's prophecy was fulfilled for these three men. The lieutenant says he held the oars in his hands but he had no strength to move them. God gave the strength and they moved and the boat moved. It moved against the current and against the wind and soon they were at the land. There they found water and coconuts and later were rescued by natives, and finally they were cared for by their own friends and brought back home.

Lieutenant Whittaker closed his talk with an unusual statement. He said that out of those twenty-one days on the life raft, those days of starving and suffering, he added two words to his vocabulary—two words that are the difference between day and night, between life and death—the two words that signify Christian faith: "I believe."

29

Woes and Windows

> *Say not ye, there are yet four months, and then cometh the harvest? Behold, I say unto you, Lift up your eyes, and look on the fields, that they are white already unto harvest.*
> —John 4:35

THE DOCTOR CAME IN A HURRY. AFTER ASKING A NUMber of questions, he tapped and thumped me here and there, took my temperature and pulse beat, listened to my lungs with his stethoscope, and then said: "We must get you to the hospital right away. You get ready to go. I'll make arrangements for the room and the ambulance."

So it was that in little more time than it takes to tell, two men came into the house with a stretcher, I was tucked in with a blanket, carried out to the ambulance, and we were on our way to the hospital. In but a few more minutes the elevator carried us to the fourth floor, I was rolled down the hall and put in a hospital bed in room number 411.

A hospital is a busy place. There are so many people there, with so many different things wrong with them. There are so many doctors and so many nurses dressed in white. There are also lots of moans and groans echoing up and down the halls for many of the patients are suffering pain, and at least once or twice a day an emergency case comes in, the ambulance siren's shrill scream heralding its coming afar off.

As I looked about in my room, I thought how small it was, just large enough for a bed, a small table, a dresser, and a couple of chairs. It seemed like a prison cell. It seemed more so when the nurse told me the rule I was to observe: "You must not get out of bed unless the doctor gives permission."

For awhile, I must admit, I felt rather blue. My freedom had been taken away from me. I could not leave until I was given permission. In fact, from now on until I was declared cured of my ills, I was to be completely taken charge of by the nurses and attendants of the hospital. Regardless of what I thought or wanted (except for very unimportant matters) decisions about me would be made by the doctor and those in charge. I must simply lie on that bed, swallow the medicine I was given, and do exactly as I was told.

Then it was that I discovered something that made everything look different. I had a window in my room! Through that window, as I lay on my bed, I could see a whole world of interesting things. There were houses where people lived and factories and office buildings where they worked. There were cars and buses, trailers and trucks, driving by. Occasionally an airplane would pass my window and often the pigeons would fly by in flocks. Coming up through the trees I saw a red kite rising. It was a very unruly kite for it kept darting and jumping around but finally it got up into the sky. Men and women, boys and girls, were walking by, some of them coming into the hospital to visit friends.

Everything in my room and in the hospital was changed for me by the magic of that window. It was interesting to look out during the daytime. It was interesting to watch the light fade in the sky in the evening and the lights go on in the houses. Some men were working late in their offices. One whole floor of the state office building was bright with light. It was fun to wonder what was going on in the different homes. Was that brightly lighted home the scene of a birthday party for the boy or girl who lived there? Were those few lights that stayed on so late the rooms where students lived? Were they studying for an examination tomorrow? And how the cars drove by! It seemed almost like a parade, except that a parade goes in just one direction. Where were all the people going and what were they going to do when they got there?

Well, I had been looking out my window a long time when I turned to read my New Testament before going to sleep. I read the story of Jesus healing and helping the people all the day long. He thought of them as God's great field of service for all who want to be God's fellow workers. He put it this way: "Say not ye, There are yet four months, and then cometh the harvest? Behold, I say unto you, Lift up your eyes, and look on the fields, that they are white already unto harvest."

Right through my hospital window I could see my field of service. This was my city, the place where I lived, and those houses out there were the homes of my fellow citizens and those offices and factories were the places where they worked. And I happened to know that it was a needy field, just as was the case in Jesus' time, for more than half the people of our city are not Christians and do not attend any of the churches. Just think, there are more boys and girls in our city who never go to Sunday school than there are who do go! There are hundreds of families who have never been inside of a church, except perhaps for a wedding. They do not know about God's love and his gracious invitation to live as members of his own family. They do not know the joy of being fellow workers with Christ in building a better community and world. They do not know the happiness of life when God is at the center of it all.

There are always so many things to thank God for that we can never make out a complete list. But that night in the hospital I thanked God for my window which helped me to see a field "white already unto harvest," and prayed a little prayer that very soon the Great Physician would heal my body and send me out as a harvester into that field for him.

30

Turning Things Right Side Up

> Jesus answered and said unto
> him, Verily, verily, I say unto
> thee, Except one be born anew,
> he cannot see the kingdom of
> God.   —John 3:3

DURING WORLD WAR II A WORD WAS USED ABOUT THE
factories and shops that meant to turn things upside
down. Since the end of the war, almost the same word
has been used with the meaning of turning things right
side up again. These words are "convert" and "recon-
vert." When the war started there was constant talk
about the conversion of industry. What was meant was
the changing of tools and dies and other pieces of machinery for the making of guns and war equipment.
Factories that had been making washing machines, re-
frigerators, automobiles, and all kinds of useful things
for our homes and our happiness, were turned into factories for making all kinds of instruments of destruction.

You know how it was. Automobile factories were
making bombing planes, machine guns, and cannon;
refrigerator plants were making fighter plane propellers;
forges were making cartridges and shells; watch factories
were making bombsights; and so on down the line. All
our machinery was working for war and the terrible
business of destroying everything useful in the enemy's
possession.

Now these same factories are reconverting or getting back to doing what they were intended to do in the first place. They are now making the useful things that make our lives more comfortable and healthful and happy. The list of these things is too long to name but it includes almost everything we use from pins and needles to houses.

The New Testament speaks of conversion and considers it a very important and necessary experience that should take place in every person's life. One time when two of the disciples on a missionary tour came to the town of Thessalonica, some bad fellows who resented their coming, said: "These that have turned the world upside down are come hither also."[1] Now Paul and Silas had not turned the world upside down, but rather, right side up, for it was in a sorry state before they came and preached Christ's gospel to the people. By preaching the gospel they helped people to understand what life is for, and they led many to dedicate themselves to Christ and his kingdom.

Everyone needs to be converted. Jesus, when talking to the scholarly teacher Nicodemus, called it being "born anew." You see, people are naturally selfish. Take a baby or a small child. He wants everything he sees, no matter whether he should have it or not. A baby will even try to pull off your nose or your ear if the fancy strikes him. There are plenty of grown-up men and women who have the same way of reaching out and taking, or trying to take, whatever looks good to them. They think only in terms of what they want and do not consider the welfare of anyone else but themselves. Such a per-

[1] Acts 17:6.

114

son shows evidence that he needs to be converted. He has continued as he was born, just a baby, snatching and grabbing whatever he wants because he has not been born again.

Selfishness is not only wanting and taking things for ourselves, but it is also using all our time and talents and money just for our own enjoyment. An unconverted person thinks that he can do whatever he pleases with his time and everything else in his possession. When he is converted, or turned right side up in his thinking, he realizes that God gave him everything he has, and God expects him to use all these things in unselfish ways, sharing them with others as well as using them for himself. A person who is right side up in his heart thinks of himself as a fellow worker with God, using his strength, his influence, and his talents and money, to help God build the kind of world where everyone can enjoy the blessings of God and all can have an opportunity to live happily.

How important it is, not only that our factories and shops should run their machinery to make useful things, but that men and women, boys and girls should have minds and hearts so in tune with God that they will use all their powers to do good and be pleasing to God in everything, every way, every day.

31

Balloons, Boasters, and Blowouts

> *For I say, through the grace*
> *that was given me, to every*
> *man that is among you, not to*
> *think of himself more highly*
> *than he ought to think; but*
> *so to think as to think soberly,*
> *according as God hath dealt to*
> *each man a measure of faith.*
> —Rom. 12:3

THE OTHER DAY I SAW SOME RUBBER BALLOONS. THEY
were the largest balloons I ever saw. Perhaps you saw
them too. The saleswoman was blowing them up with a
vacuum cleaner, the hose attached to the opposite end
so that the air came out instead of being sucked in.
At first these balloons were little shriveled up bits of
rubber, but as the air filled them they became so large
they were at least a yard in diameter. But the most interesting part of it was the faces painted on the balloons
and the figures they made. Some were made to look like
men's faces, some like rabbits, and some like pigs.

I guess it was because of the faces that I began to
think of a boy I know. He blows himself up like a balloon. Yes, that is just about what he does. He says:
"Why I can do that and that and that." From the way
he brags you would think there is not anything he cannot do if you just gave him a little time.

While I was thinking about the balloons and the boy together, it occurred to me how quickly a balloon will deflate if you stick a pin in it. Of course you have tried that little trick. The balloon pops and explodes like a firecracker, it bursts so fast.

Of course my friend who tells the big tales would not burst or explode if he were pricked with a pin, but there are some kinds of pricks that would make him very small indeed. When one talks big about something he knows little or nothing about, and someone who really knows a lot about that subject comes along, it makes the first fellow feel like he would like to crawl in a hole somewhere—and pull the hole in after him, as we say. When a boy tells how good a baseball player he is and then he gets a chance to show what he can do, and finds all the other boys are as good or better than he, then he begins to wish down in his heart that he had not talked so loud. And it doesn't pay to brag about one's importance either, for we usually find that if we are absent for some reason or another, things go on just about as well as if we had been there, for someone else takes our place and does just as good a job as we would have done—perhaps even better.

The letter to the Romans has something to say about boasters, and about blowouts too: "For I say, through the grace that was given me, to every man that is among you, not to think of himself more highly than he ought to think; but so to think as to think soberly, according as God hath dealt to each man a measure of faith."

Paul knew that a blowout was sure to come to a boasting man, and of course he included boys and girls too, for men and women are just boys and girls grown taller and older. Yet Paul did not expect us to shrivel up, underrate our abilities, and be ashamed of ourselves. He continually preached to people to believe in themselves and undertake big things. He even challenged them to tackle the impossible sometimes. He himself sounded as if he were boasting when he said: "I can do all things." But Paul did not stop there. He added: "In him that strengtheneth me." [1] Yes, it is Christ who makes the difference. We can be confident and proud if we are boasting of Christ; but we must be very humble when talking of ourselves. With Christ's help, we can, like Paul, do all things.

If we want to do any boasting, let us boast about our Christ, the King of Kings and Lord of Lords.

[1] Phil. 4:13

32

I Must!

> *From that time began Jesus to show unto his disciples, that he must go unto Jerusalem, and suffer many things.*
> —Matt. 16:21

THE CROSS OF CHRIST HAS BEEN CALLED A MYSTERY. It is true that no one can fully explain it. It means so much to the whole world that the wisest of men have not been able to comprehend it. Boys and girls can understand something of its meaning, however, and every time we try to understand more it makes our lives bigger and better.

The very spirit of Jesus, as he went to Jerusalem knowing that he must be crucified there, is part of the meaning of the cross. Jesus told his disciples that he "must go unto Jerusalem, and suffer many things of the elders and chief priests and scribes, and be killed." The disciples did not want Jesus to get into trouble and they tried to prevent him from going to Jerusalem. Peter stood right in front of him in the road and said: "Be it far from thee, Lord: this shall never be unto thee." But Jesus answered Peter as though he were the terrible Tempter and said: "Get thee behind me, Satan: thou art a stumbling-block unto me: for thou mindest not the things of God, but the things of men."

Then Jesus explained to his disciples that there are certain things that men should do because God wants these things done. The law does not require them and often people do not want them, but if God wants them, good men will do God's will even if it costs them their lives. Brave men of God have always said: "If it is God's will, I will do it, cost what it may!"

Have you heard the story of Dr. Claude H. Barlow, of Cairo, Egypt? He is one of those heroes who said, "I must." Dr. Barlow, as a young man, went to be the missionary doctor in the American hospital at Shaosing, China. There he found a dreadful disease causing the Chinese to die by the thousand. By examination of many bodies he discovered tiny parasites, or flukes, in the intestines. But where the flukes came from and how persons contracted the disease was unknown.

The laboratory facilities in Shaosing were very meager, but Dr. Barlow was determined to find the source of infection of this disease. He thought of bringing a sick Chinese to the United States for the American doctors to study his case, but the government would not allow this to be done. There was another course that could be taken—a desperate one—and Dr. Barlow decided to take it. "One Sunday morning," he says, "when most of the assistants were at the church service, I took thirty-two of the flukes from the body of a patient in the hospital and drank them down." He did not tell any of his helpers, not even his wife. Then he took a ship for the United States.

Some weeks later Dr. Barlow appeared at Johns Hopkins University and told the amazed doctors what he had done. They gladly took him as their patient and succeeded in relieving him of the deadly parasites. The story has a happy ending, for Dr. Barlow lived and remained in the hospital laboratory to study the flukes to determine their life cycle and discover how they enter the human body. He learned the secret, finding that a certain kind of snail acts as host for the miracidia which produce the flukes. With this knowledge he was able to take measures to protect the Chinese against the disease.

This thrilling story can be briefly told, but it took many long months to accomplish and it meant much toil and great pain and suffering for Dr. Barlow. Even after going back to China it was necessary for him to contract the disease several times before he could complete his experiments. Many times he risked death, but he felt it was worth taking the chance. No one knows how many Chinese lives have been saved from death because Dr. Barlow, God's physician, said: "If God wants it done, I must!"

Another story begins in the Philippine Islands. On December 20, 1943, eleven of our faithful missionaries and one little boy, son of one of the missionary families, were killed by the Japanese on Panay. These missionaries had been hiding in caves up in the mountains, and when they were found, after the Japanese invaded the Philippines, they were declared to be spies and were given just one hour to prepare for death. The missionaries spent that hour in prayer and singing hymns of worship to God. Then the terrible blow came and all were killed.

Two of the people killed that fateful day were James Howard Covell and his wife, missionaries who had been working in Japan and had gone to the Philippines when the war started between Japan and the United States. One of their daughters is Margaret Covell Struble. When Mrs. Struble received the terrible news of the death of her father and mother she was stricken with grief. As she thought more and more of the tragedy, she thought more and more of the great need of the Japanese people to know God and his love. She thought of the faith of her father and mother and their lives of service in the interest of good will and peace. She remembered the slogan they used to stamp on their letters: "Friendships not Battleships." So Mrs. Struble sought an opportunity to carry on in her own way the work of her father and mother. She said to herself, "*I must* do my part to help build a bridge of friendship"; and she became a worker in a Japanese relocation center near Denver and ministered to the Japanese in our own country.

Dr. Barlow and Mrs. Struble help us to understand the spirit of the cross and the meaning of Christ when he said: "If any man would come after me, let him deny himself, and take up his cross, and follow me." [1]

[1] Matt. 16:24.

33

Lilies and Life

> *Be not fashioned according to this world: but be ye transformed by the renewing of your mind.* —Rom. 12:2

Lilies have a great story for us on Easter Sunday morning. We always see them at Easter time and expect them to be in the stores and in our homes and at the church. But did you ever realize that they actually tell the Easter message?

Let us take a good look at an Easter lily. We will need to take off the fancy wrapping around the pot if we want to see a very important part of the lily and understand an important part of what the lily has to say. When we take off the silver-colored paper we find an ugly earthen pot. Inside the pot we see some plain black dirt. We will not dig in the dirt for all of us know that deep down there is the lily bulb. It looks very much like an onion. The bulb lives down there in the darkness and every day water must be poured into the pot to keep the lily alive. We do not often think of the bulb when we look at a lily, but if it were not for the bulb we would have no beautiful white lily at all.

Then there is the green stalk with its bright green leaves and the lovely gay white lilies themselves. If you look at an Easter lily with your imagination as well as your eyes, you can see how much these lilies resemble trumpets. The lily plant seems to be blowing trumpets of praise announcing the joyous Easter day. These lilies also look like bells ringing out the good news in all directions.

With the bulb in the dirt and the white blossoms high above, a lily lives in two worlds. Yes, the bulb is in the world of earth and the flower is in the world of sunshine and fresh air. Though the bulb is buried in the earth, it does not live there alone for it sends up shoots into the sunshine and becomes truly beautiful in its second world.

Did you ever think of the fact that you and I also live in two worlds? Our two worlds are not dirt and sunshine, but the world of physical things and the world of spiritual things. We live in our bodies which must be fed and clothed and kept warm from the winter's cold. Because our bodies must be cared for if we are to be well and happy, we spend a lot of time with physical things. But the other world in which we live is even more important. It is the world of beautiful thoughts and ideals, the world of righteousness and truth, peace and love. We can actually think God's thoughts after him and live in such a lovely way that we cause him to be pleased with us.

Jesus said to his disciples: "I am the way, and the truth, and the life." [1] His way was the way of love. He was always loving people and doing kind things for them. He never hurt anyone or made any one unhappy. He always helped them and brought them good cheer. He used to say that even if people are bad to you, strike you or snub you or make fun of you, you must

[1] John 14:6.

124

not treat them that way. Rather you must return good for evil and treat them as you would *like* to have them treat you. "Turn the other cheek," he said, and "pray for them that persecute you." [2]

But Jesus' way was not the way most people were living. In fact, he seemed to be the only one traveling that way. He was blazing a new trail in right living. Most people were selfish and greedy. They grabbed what they wanted and fought with one another and quarreled and hated and were very bad indeed. It was because the whole world was full of wickedness that Jesus was crucified at last. There on the cross it looked like hate and selfishness were stronger than love and service. But Easter morning came and the triumphant announcement of the angel: "He is not here, but is risen." [3] Yes, Jesus' way is the way of victory and of life. That is the great truth of Easter.

The Easter lily tells a wonderful story. It tells us that life can be beautiful. We need not live just in the physical world of things but we can reach up into the world of God's truth and love, blossoming out in loveliness ourselves. We can walk the way of Jesus. We can live so nobly and so grandly that God will be proud of us and we shall go on with him forever.

[2] Matt. 5:44.   [3] Luke 24:6.

Signs of Spring# 34

Signs of Spring

*The invisible things of him
since the creation of the world
are clearly seen, being perceived
through the things that are
made, even his everlasting
power and divinity.*
—Rom. 1:20

SPRING MUST BE JUST AROUND THE CORNER. THE robins have been back for weeks, but of course some people say there are always a few robins around. They stay in the evergreens and in protected places and then come out the first day that is warm and sunshiny. Kites have been in the sky too for quite a while, and boys and girls have been roller skating on the sidewalk. Today, though, I saw some infallible signs of spring. The boys were batting out balls on the baseball lot and the girls were jumping rope on the street. Some college students were playing tennis, at least one golfer was practicing on his front lawn, and men were standing on the street corner in little groups, just talking. I did not see any marble games or tops, but certainly they must be happening somewhere in town for the feel of spring is in the air.

I know there are still piles of dirty snow in shady places and it is still crisp and cold at night. But spring is on the way, and it won't be long now! I suppose the surest sign is when mother decides to clean house and then everybody at home knows the real thing is here!

In a few days, or weeks at most, the first crocuses will push up through the soft wet earth and open their bright smiling little cup-like faces, and then will come the daffodils and the violets and we will want to take a stroll in the woods and pick wild flowers and hear the frogs croak and see the butterflies and bees flitting and humming on their merry way.

Then the green leaves will appear and the great ghost trees will no longer stand like forsaken dead things but will blossom into life. The squirrels will scamper around, the birds will be building their nests and singing all day long, the ducks and geese will be flying overhead on their northbound journey, and the boys and girls coming home from high school will be holding hands!

But spring is more than green leaves, flowers, and returning birds. It is more than outdoor games and lovers walking slowly by. It is a new feeling deep down inside and a new happiness within our very souls. It is the voice of God whispering to us through the rebirth of the great out of doors, and a stirring in our own hearts in answer to nature's invitation to come out into the sunshine and the beauty of an awakening world.

God speaks to us in many ways. We read his word in the Bible. Prophets, apostles, and men of God through the years have written down the great truths of God that have been made known to them. God speaks to us in the life and words of Christ, and especially in his cross and resurrection. God speaks to us in our own consciences as we know deep within us what we ought to do and what we ought not to do. God speaks to us through our parents and our teachers, both by what they tell us and by what they do day after day. God speaks to us in music and in art. When we hear great music or see a wonderful painting it causes us to think seriously, and often to "think God's thoughts after him."

Paul was undoubtedly speaking of the voice of nature and springtime telling us about God when he wrote to the Romans: "The invisible things of him since the creation of the world are clearly seen, being perceived through the things that are made, even his everlasting power and divinity."

At first that verse appears difficult. Paul says that invisible things are seen. Certainly they are. When the buds burst on the bushes and trees and the spring flowers push up through the ground, we see them and, because they do come, we know that some invisible power—even God's power—is behind them. We see God in the things he does in nature. We cannot actually see God himself but we can see amazing things happening that only God could do. So we see God through his wonderful works.

Springtime, then, is a time for praising God and thanking him for his gifts that fill every day full to the brim.

> Bless Jehovah, O my soul;
> And all that is within me, bless his holy name.
> Bless Jehovah, O my soul,
> And forget not all his benefits.[1]

[1] Ps. 103:1-2.

35

Be Prepared!

Watch therefore: for ye know not on what day your Lord cometh. —Matt. 24:42

A CROWD HAD GATHERED AROUND THE HIGH-SCHOOL building and I wandered over that way to see what was going on. Several fire trucks were there: the long ladder truck, the hose truck, and the chief's red car. Besides these, there was another special truck with a motion-picture machine mounted and ready for action.

It did not take long to find out what it was all about. The fire department was demonstrating a new fire escape gadget it had just recently acquired. It was a long canvas slide called an "evacuator," which the firemen fastened securely to a third-story window and then asked a number of boys and girls to leave the building by way of the window and the slide. It was lots of fun, at least it seemed to be, for the boys and girls were enjoying it and all of them in the crowd wanted to have a try at the slippery slide too.

Yes, that contraption was very much like a slide in a playground except that it was very much longer. One end was bolted to the window sill and the other end was held by half a dozen firemen. Then the boys and girls just sat down on the window sill and slid down the slide to the ground. After quite a number had gone down they allowed some of the boys to try other positions. Instead of sitting down they lay down on their backs and came down the slide head first. Then they wrapped one girl in a blanket as though she were a casualty case and started her down the slide head first. This did not work so well for, as she slid down into the sagging canvas, her body bent over and she turned a somersault backward. By good fortune she landed in the arms of the firemen, but she might have fallen over the side of the chute and been badly hurt. After this the firemen were more careful about the position of those coming down. With care they were able to send a large number down in a very short time. Even the crippled janitor came down. First he sent his crutches down and then came sliding after them.

While all this was going on the cameramen were working. One was operating the camera on the truck, parked quite a distance from the building to allow a view of the crowd as well as the building and the evacuator. Another man was on the roof taking shots of the boys and girls as they came down. Later this man came down to the window and put on quite a performance by hanging to the window by one leg as he took more pictures of the scene.

Someone suggested that there should be some smoke pouring out of the window to make it look more realistic when the movies were taken, but the important thing was the fact that these boys and girls and the firemen were practicing to be prepared in case of emergency. We will hope that none of those boys and girls ever need to come out of a burning building by way of a canvas slide, but it is better to know how to do it and be prepared for anything that may happen. That is the reason we take first-aid training and life-saving training and learn to do a great many things that we sincerely hope we will never need to do because of actual accidents or calamities. During the war we had air-raid drills and black-out tests and thousands of people in every community were drilled to work in teams with other people at a moment's notice. First-aid stations were set up in churches, lodges, and store buildings, and persons with training were assigned to these stations and were supposed to rush to their posts at once when the siren sounded. We never had an air raid in the United States and there was no practical need for all this training, but it was much better to have had the preparation and not use it than to have had no preparation at all.

Sometimes boys or girls wonder what is the use of studying arithmetic or geography or some other subject at school. They may also wonder why mother asks them to assume some responsibility at home and take time from their free hours to work around the house. All of these things are important. There is nothing good we can learn that is not useful. It all goes into our fund of stored up knowledge and skill, preparing us to meet all kinds of situations and do what needs to be done when the time comes.

Jesus believed in being prepared and told his disciples: "Watch therefore: for ye know not on what day your Lord cometh." Like a savings account in the bank, like a parachute in a damaged plane, like K rations in the wilderness is the knowledge and skill stored away in mind and hand ready to be used in time of emergency. The Boy Scout motto is a good one: "Be Prepared!"

36

Home Defense

No one can enter into the house of the strong man, and spoil his goods, except he first bind the strong man; and then he will spoil his house.
—Mark 3:27

SATURDAY WAS THE OPENING OF THE TROUT FISHING season. I had thought a good deal about the possibilities of getting out for at least part of the day, but all the trout streams I knew about were so far away that it would take hours and hours to reach them, and I just could not neglect my work all day Saturday. You can imagine my surprise and delight when a friend telephoned Friday night and baited me with a series of questions: "How would you like to go fishing tomorrow?" Of course I wanted to go but it was no use talking about such a thing. It was imposible. "Would you go if you knew a good place just twenty-five miles away?" Would I! I would have gone twice that far for a real chance to catch some rainbow or brook trout. "Then I will let you in on a little secret. I know a place just ten miles from the city. They say the fish there run as large as three or four pounds."

You can easily guess the result of that telephone conversation. I made arrangements to get started on a fishing trip next morning long before daylight, and I got busy at once getting my tackle ready for an early start.

We will pass over the preliminaries and the early rising and even the fishing. I don't mean that the fishing was not interesting and that it was not successful, for it was both. But on that fishing trip I had an experience even more interesting than fishing, and that is what I want to tell you about.

While I was busily fishing I heard the whistle of wings and two teal ducks alighted on the water not more than a hundred yards from where I stood. It was a beautiful sight. I watched them for some time. After awhile they flew away and then it was that I noticed a big goose standing like a statue on the edge of a brook that fed the pond in which I was fishing. I looked again and again to be sure my eyes were not playing tricks on me, for I did not know that there were any wild geese in that neighborhood. Sure enough he was real: a wild Canada goose.

Immediately I became more interested in the goose than in my fishing. I wondered why he did not take to the air and fly away when he saw me. I started walking toward him to see how close I could get before he would fly. I had not gone ten feet toward that goose when he suddenly began honking at the top of his voice, working his neck toward me like a snake, and coming straight at me! Imagine such a thing: a wild Canada goose, one of the most wary of wild fowl, apparently preparing to attack me instead of making his escape.

Then it occurred to me that this old gander must be protecting his mate on a nest in the near-by territory. I stood perfectly still and carefully scanned the ground on all sides. After minutes of careful search I discovered the nest and the mother goose sitting upon it. It was just some twigs covered with down from the goose's own body, and it was right on the ground in the open, with no protection of rock or brush. The goose was trying to make herself unnoticed by lying perfectly still. Her neck and head were resting on the ground. She was motionless but I could see her sharp, black beady eyes following my every move.

I did not disturb the two geese but I know just what that gander would have done had I gone closer to the nest. He would have come at me hissing and blowing and would not have hesitated a second to grab me by the leg and bite hard enough to make me sorry I ever came that way. No doubt the mother goose would have then joined him and the two would have put up such a battle that I would have retreated on the run.

Those two geese taught me something about home. They reminded me of a word Jesus once said: "No one can enter into the house of the strong man, and spoil his goods, except he first bind the strong man; and then he will spoil his house."

Even wary wild birds become fearless when their home is endangered. They forget their own safety and lay down their lives if need be to protect their nest and their young. "Home" is said to be the sweetest word in any language, and I believe it must be sweet even in the language of a goose.

37

Tribute to Mother

*Having been reminded of the
unfeigned faith that is in thee;
which dwelt first in thy grand-
mother Lois, and thy mother
Eunice; and, I am persuaded,
in thee also.* —II Tim. 1:5

THE MOST FAMOUS PICTURE ANY ARTIST EVER PAINTED
of his own mother was done by James Abbott McNeill
Whistler. This picture is now hanging in the Louvre
in Paris. It has traveled far and wide and appeared on
a United States postage stamp issued in recognition of
Mother's Day. It is the best-known picture of a mother
ever painted, though it was not even called a picture
of his mother by the artist. Whistler simply named it
"Arrangement in Gray and Black." But it was his own
mother whose portrait he painted, and the whole world
came to know it, to admire it, and to make it a sort of
universal symbol of motherhood.

To understand the picture we need to know something about Whistler's parents as well as himself. His
father was an army officer and a railroad engineer. He
did not operate locomotives but he constructed railroads.
When James—or "Jemie," as his father and mother
called him—was born the family lived in Lowell,
Massachusetts. His father was building a railroad from
Lowell to Boston. When that job was finished he moved

to Connecticut, where he had another railroad contract, and then to Springfield, Massachusetts, still building railroads—mapping out the route, surveying the grades, building the bridges, and all the many other things that are necessary in order to lay the rails so the trains can run.

One day two distinguished visitors came to Springfield and they went to Jemie's home. They had come to see his father. I presume all the boys and girls of the neighborhood were excited about these strangers and gathered in little groups and asked questions. This was because they were army colonels and they came from Russia. Their mission was to ask Major Whistler to go to Russia and help them build a railroad from St. Petersburg to Moscow. After a great deal of thought about the matter the major accepted the job and so it was that young Jemie, about a year later, went with his mother and brothers to join their father and live in St. Petersburg (now known as Leningrad).

A sad experience came to the Whistler family there, for the father died and the mother and children came back to the United States. Jemie's mother was a brave woman and courageously faced her sorrow and the hard task of raising her children alone. She was a very religious person and lived by faith. She said: "I shall not faint but labor, and pray the blessing of God upon my endeavors."

It was because of his mother's determination and faith that Jemie was able to get the fine education he received, and was inspired to work hard and study hard to prepare himself to become one of the world's greatest artists. He studied in Paris and in London. He studied the methods and the paintings of artists of many lands, for he wanted to learn all he could about color and drawing and was eager to get help from the great artists of the world.

Though Whistler's mother was not an artist she really influenced him more than any of his art teachers, and it was natural that he should honor her by painting her picture as his tribute of love and appreciation for her.

But Jemie knew that painting his mother's picture was no easy task. He had been trying to draw and paint since he was a very small boy. One day when he was only four or five years of age his mother found him under the table, and she said: "Jemie, what are you doing there under the table?" Jemie replied: "Just drawin', Mummy." Yes, he was just drawing, even then. When he was about thirteen or fourteen years of age his father suggested that he paint a picture of his mother. You see, Jemie's father was not only an engineer but he was a pretty good artist too, and he had painted a picture of his own mother when he was only thirteen. It was a pretty good picture too. So Jemie tried to sketch his mother but found it a very difficult thing to do. He said to his father: "I can't paint a picture of Mummy; it is a lot easier to draw Bossy" (the cow). So he practiced and worked on other subjects to be better prepared before he tried that important picture of his mother.

It was not until James Whistler had became a skillful and famous artist that he attempted to paint his mother's picture. It is truly a great picture for he painted not only his mother's features but her very character as well, as only a son could do who knew and loved

137

her. It is a great painter's tribute to a wonderful mother.

On Mother's Day we sing songs about mother, recite poems, and wear a flower in her honor. We probably remember to give her a little gift too. But did you ever think that the finest tribute we can possibly give to our mother—and the gift that will make her happiest—is just to be the kind of boy or girl she wants us to be?

38

Mud Pies That Talk

Being made manifest that ye are
an epistle of Christ, ministered
by us, written not with ink,
but with the Spirit of the living
God; not in tables of stone,
but in tables that are hearts
of flesh. —II Cor. 3:3

WHOEVER HEARD OF A BOY OR GIRL WHO NEVER IN HIS whole life made a mud pie? I suppose boys and girls everywhere make mud pies and put them in the sun to dry and harden. Can't you see a row of pies now: big pies, little pies, and all sorts of funny-shaped pies?

Of all the pies you have made and have seen, did you ever know of one that could talk? Of course you remember the Mother Goose rhyme about the blackbirds in the king's pie:

Sing a song of sixpence,
A pocket full of rye;
Four-and-twenty blackbirds
Baked in a pie!

When the pie was opened
The birds began to sing;
Was not that a dainty dish
To set before the king?

That must have been a very musical pie, but I know of hundreds of little pies, made by people thousands of years ago, that tell stories. They talk a very peculiar language but scholars who have learned how to read the language report very interesting things they have learned from the "talking mud pies."

These talking pies are clay tablets used by the Sumerians at least five thousand years ago. The cities where these people lived are buried under sand and dust now. If you were to travel in the land of Irak today, you would notice little plateaus or elevated tables of land rising a little higher than the surrounding plain. These mounds would probably cover buried cities.

Some of these buried cities have been dug up, and in addition to the houses and public buildings and temples, many unusual monuments and statues have been found. There are images of lions, elephants, and winged bulls, as well as pictures of people working or playing or worshiping, and of course there are lots of vases, jars, and small ornaments. However, more important than all of these objects are the little mud pies that talk, for by reading them scholars can understand the meaning of all the rest. They tell the story of the people who lived so long ago.

In order to understand the peculiar marks and read them it was necessary to find the key. I suppose this search was much like the problem our government men had during the war in cracking the German and Japanese codes. It took scholars with special preparation, men who knew many languages and were especially good at solving puzzles.

It seems that the Sumerians and the Assyrians and Babylonians, who lived before the time of Abraham, had the habit of writing on little clay bricks. A scribe would take a piece of soft clay out of his bucket and sit down to write a letter or record a business deal or make a note of something that happened that day. This clay was somewhat like the modeling clay you use to make animals and toy houses. The scribe, however, did not use his fingers to shape his clay tablet. He used a stylus or stick with a sharp edge at the end. It made an impression that looked very much like a nail lying flat. To write his note or letter the scribe would make many marks with his stylus, putting several marks together at different angles and in varied combinations, some up and down, some slanting, and some horizontal. This was the way these ancient people made letters and words. It was their printing.

Some very important things have been learned from the talking pies. You see, the people who wrote on clay lived before, and also during, the time of many of our Old Testament characters. The Bible stories of these characters are usually very brief and we would like to know much more about them and the way people lived in those days. So it is that these clay records add many side lights to the Bible stories.

The scholars who have learned to read the story of the clay tablets tell us they are very glad indeed that these Sumerians wrote on clay instead of on paper because paper would have crumbled to dust in five thousand years. In some of the tombs they found skeletons of kings and other royal people. They were once clothed in fine garments but now the cloth has completely vanished except for a little dust. Only the gold or silver buttons, or pins that once held the clothing together, are left to show that there was clothing when the bodies were placed in the tomb. But every clay tablet or talking pie is just as sound as it was when first written and placed in the sun to dry. In fact it gets harder as the years go by and becomes like rock or flint.

I wonder if Paul was thinking of these clay bricks when he said that each of us is a letter of Christ (telling the good news to all who meet us), "Written not with ink, but with the Spirit of the living God; not in tables of stone, but in tables that are hearts of flesh."

39

The Road to Greatness

*I have been crucified with
Christ; and it is no longer I
that live, but Christ liveth in
me.* —Gal. 2:20

JASCHA HEIFETZ CAME TO OUR CITY. EVERYONE WHO
could borrow, buy, or beg a ticket went to hear him.
Not only the music lovers went but the curious as well,
for everyone wanted to see and hear the world's greatest
living violinist.

Here is a man, forty-five years of age, who has traveled about one million, seven hundred thousand miles
(a distance greater than seven trips to the moon!) and
has played over seventy-five thousand hours in his life.
He has made four world tours and each year tours the
United States and Canada. During the last war he
played for the armed forces in camps and hospitals and
made three trips overseas.

What is so wonderful about this great Heifetz? To
see him on the street you probably would not be im-
pressed with his appearance. There is nothing unusual
about him physically. He does not even wear his hair
long and shaggy as many musicians do. He is of medium
size. He is just a nice-appearing man.

You see, Heifetz is more than just himself. There is
something additional, something under his chin and
held in his delicate fingers. It takes a violin to complete

Heifetz and make him what he is today. He carries two famous and priceless violins with him, but these violins would be of little value in your hands or mine. It is the combination that counts—this man Heifetz and his wonderful violin. Without the violin he is just an ordinary man. He is not an orator or a singer or a poet. He needs his violin to be great.

It is said that Heifetz does not like publicity about himself. He explains that he will say what needs to be said with his violin. He does not want to give his opinion on this subject or that, or tell some story about his travels; he prefers just to pour out his soul in music.

It is true that Heifetz has an unusual life history but he likes to sum it up briefly: "Born in Russia, first lesson at three, debut in Russia at five, debut in New York in 1917." Short, isn't it? Such a person as Heifetz does not need a build-up. When he is on the concert stage with his violin you know the master violinist is there and you do not ask any questions. You just sit back in wonder and listen to his charming music.

This world-famed musician, both in his great playing and in his attitude of humility, exemplifies the secret of true greatness. A man becomes so much a part of some great force that he and the force are one. Heifetz and music are one. To all who know music his name means the best in violin technique. People cannot think of either Heifetz or violin music without thinking of the other. They belong together.

This is a law of life. Think of any great man you choose, and at the same time you think of that man you will think of the great cause or ideal he championed. Take a few names and see how this works. Beethoven means music; Michelangelo means art; Shakespeare means plays; Spurgeon means great preaching; Livingstone means missions; Washington means our country; Edison means electrical invention; Robert Raikes means the Sunday school; George Williams means the Y.M.C.A.; Clara Barton means the Red Cross; Lincoln means emancipation of slaves; Columbus means America. We could go on and on. Great lives are men and women so closely connected with a great cause as to be lost in that cause, giving themselves wholeheartedly and completely to it and living for it.

In the second chapter of Galatians, Paul expressed the meaning of the Christian life in just such terms. He spoke of himself and said: "I have been crucified with Christ; and it is no longer I that live, but Christ liveth in me."

Can you think of Paul without thinking of Christ? Paul is our greatest teacher of Christ. He teaches us not just by what he has written in the New Testament in his many epistles or letters, but he himself is his greatest sermon, for his life is a great and noble example of Christlikeness.

Sometimes a group of boys and girls is asked this question: What do you expect to become when you grow up? Most boys and girls have been thinking about that question and have some idea in mind. I doubt if any one of you has been thinking about becoming great. You want to be a grocer, a doctor, a lawyer, a minister, an aviator, and so forth. Perhaps none of you will ever be world-famous and then again you may be. Greatness is a matter of distance along the road. Everyone should be on the road to greatness and going in the right direction. Some will be miles ahead of the rest and they are the outstanding or famous ones. Regardless of our special work or profession, all of us should aspire to be good Christians, if not great ones. We will achieve that, just as Paul did, by deciding that we will so live that each day there will be less and less of us appearing, and more and more of Christ, until some day we can truly say: "It is no longer I that live, but Christ liveth in me."

40

A New New Testament

> *Give diligence to present thyself approved unto God, a workman that needeth not to be ashamed, handling aright the word of truth.*
>
> —II Tim. 2:15

IN COLUMBUS, OHIO, THERE WAS A GREAT MEETING OF church leaders and the high point was the presentation of a new New Testament. This took place at the annual meeting of the International Council of Religious Education. Twelve hundred delegates representing forty different denominations were there from all over the United States and Canada. For about twelve years a committee of scholars had been working on a new version of the New Testament and during this convention the chairman of the New Testament committee, Dean Luther A. Weigle of the Yale Divinity School, presented the first copy of the new book to the president of the International Council, Harold E. Stassen, former governor of Minnesota.

Why did we need a *new* New Testament?

If we go back to the earliest days of the New Testament, we will see that we have had many new New Testaments. At first, of course, the New Testament was not a book at all as we know it now, but a number of books, or rather scrolls. These scrolls, in the earliest days, were not even all together. For instance, Paul's letters to the Corinthians were in the church at Corinth. His letter to the Romans was in Rome. His letter to the Ephesians was in the church at Ephesus, and so forth. What happened was that Christians in those days realized how helpful and valuable all these writings were and all the churches wanted all the letters. So the churches sent copies of their letters to each other until all the churches had all the letters. Even then there was just a set of scrolls in each church, not a book, and all were written by hand on parchment, a writing material made of the skin of an animal, usually a sheep or goat.

If we had a copy of these scrolls today, just as each of the early churches had, not a one of us here could read a word of the letters. You see, they were written in Greek.

First of all, a New Testament was needed that was all in one piece, and second, it was needed to be written in a language the common people could read. It took hundreds of years for this to be done, and men lost their lives because they insisted it should be done. This is hard for us to understand today for we believe that everyone should have a New Testament and everyone should read and study it regularly if he would be a good Christian.

The first Bible that was all in one piece, containing both the books of the Old Testament and the New, was known as the Vulgate. It was entirely written by hand with a pen, and was written in Latin. You see, it was thought by the church leaders that only the priests who knew Latin should read the Bible, and they would tell the people what they needed to know. So you and I could not have read and understood that first Bible even if we had had a chance to take it into our own hands.

If we jump over a thousand years and come to the first New Testament in English, we still would have difficulty reading it, for it was old-fashioned English and almost as hard to read as a foreign language. This English translation was made by John Wycliffe, and he was greatly criticized for making it since the priests and the scholars of the church called English a "vulgar" language and said the Bible should be written only in Latin, which they considered a "holy" language.

Then one hundred years later came the first printing press. The first book printed was a Bible, but it was a Latin Bible.

The story of the first printed English Bible is a thrilling one but it ended in tragedy for the hero. William Tyndale was martyred for his trouble, but what a brave scholar he was! Not finding a place in all England where he could quietly work on a translation of the Bible into English, he went to Germany. Even there, after finishing his translation and starting his printing press, he was discovered and forced to flee. Finally he succeeded in printing an English Bible and sent it to England in sacks of flour, bales of cloth, and cases of merchandise. This was necessary because the officials of the church were watching for this English Bible and every copy they could find they burned. Finally they caught Tyndale himself and burned him at the stake. The Bible had been given to the people in a language they could read and understand, but at a terrible cost. We should remember this and always count the English Bible as one of the greatest and most precious of all our blessings.

The first great English Bible to be authorized and allowed to be sold to anyone wishing to buy it was the King James Bible printed in 1611. This is the Bible you most frequently see today and it is perhaps the best-loved of all the translations and editions. It is not a modern Bible, however. It is written in the language of Shakespeare and often we do not understand the meaning of the words. That is one reason why it was thought necessary to have a revision of the Bible about eighty years ago. Another reason was the discovery of some very old manuscripts that enabled scholars to make a fresh study of the original texts. Now they did not need to work with Greek and Hebrew texts that themselves were copies of copies of the original writings, but they could study three of the earliest copies of the original texts. This led to the printing of the Revised Version which we know as the American Revised or Standard Version of the Bible.

But language seems to be a living thing just as people who use it are living, and it keeps growing and the meanings of words change with their use. So a new revision was needed. This is the reason for the new New Testament just given us by the nine scholars working for the International Council of Religious Education.

Here are some of the interesting changes in this new New Testament. First of all, it reads like other books. I mean it is in paragraphs that can be read without all the verse numbers getting in the way. The verse numbers are there but printed very small. Do you know how the verse numbers came to be in our New Testaments? It is an interesting story. A printer named Robert Stephens was riding on a horse from Paris to Lyons in

1551. He was thinking of the problem he had in correcting mistakes in his printing of the Bible. It was difficult to find the words since the lines were not numbered and he had to count the words from the beginning of a chapter to find the mistake. So he proceeded to mark the chapters into verses as he was jogging along on the back of his horse! That was an amazing accomplishment! It is most amazing that the same verse numbers continue to this day!

Another thing you will notice about your new New Testament is the use of "you" instead of "thee," "thou," and "ye." The language is the language we are accustomed to reading in modern books and magazines.

The revisers changed certain words to make them better understood. Just to take a few samples: In the King James Version we read in John 14:2 "In my Father's house are many mansions." It has always been hard to see how a house could have many other houses inside for to us a mansion is a whole house. The new version, instead of "mansions," uses the word "rooms." We can understand that better. In John 15:2, the new version uses the word "prunes," which is certainly better understood in connection with cutting off branches than the word "purgeth," as is used in the King James Version.

One final word. The new translation, in the well-known text of Paul written to Timothy—where the King James Version says, "Study to show thyself approved," and the Standard Version says, "Give diligence" —says simply, "Do your best." This is a fine challenge for all of us: *Do your best* to be pleasing to God in all ways, always.

41

Wanted: Boys and Girls

*He said, certainly I will be
with thee.* —Exod. 3:12

I'M SURE ALL YOU BOYS AND GIRLS HAVE SEEN A SIGN
reading: "Boy Wanted," or perhaps: "Girl Wanted."
You may have seen it in a store window downtown. A
boy was needed to deliver packages during the Christmas
season, or a girl was needed to run errands on Saturdays.
There are many places where boys and girls are useful
and there are many things which you can do both at
home and elsewhere.

Did you ever see a sign reading: "God Wants Boy and
Girl"? Probably you never did but the statement is
true. We could put it in even stronger terms: "God
Needs Boy and Girl." That may seem to be an exaggera-
tion but it is not. As we think how great God is and how
powerful and wonderful, it may seem as though you and
I could not possibly be of any real use to him. That may
be the way we look at it, but it is not the way God looks
at it.

In Old Testament times a tiny baby was saved in
an unusual way. The king of Egypt had ordered all
the boy babies killed, but this baby's mother made a
little basket boat for him and sent him floating on the
Nile River. You remember how Pharaoh's daughter
found him and took him to be her own child, and how

she called him Moses, which means "Drawer-out," for, she said: "I drew him out of the water."

It was to this same Moses, now a man—in fact, a rather old man—that God came because he needed just such a man to help him save the people of Israel from their slavery in Egypt. Moses was tending his father-in-law's sheep on the plain and he saw an amazing sight. A bush was burning but it did not burn up. You know how quickly a small bush will burn if it is dry enough to burn at all. It seems to go up in a puff. It just cracks and pops and then it is nothing but black twigs and ashes.

Naturally Moses was curious when the bush kept burning, so he walked over closer to see it better. Then it was that he realized that God was attracting his attention, and he reverently took off his shoes, as was the custom in those days when one came into the presence of some great person. Then as he stood there with his head bowed, God said: "Come now therefore, and I will send thee unto Pharaoh, that thou mayest bring forth my people the children of Israel out of Egypt." [1]

It is easy for us today to see that Moses was just the man for such an undertaking. He knew the Egyptians, for he had lived in the palace of the king for forty years. He also knew the wilderness and could help the people when they must pass through the open country and live in tents for months and years. He himself had lived in the wilderness for forty years. Since we know the story and how it ends, we know Moses was just the man God needed, but Moses, that day by the burning

[1] Exod. 3:10.

bush, was bashful or humble, and he could not understand how God could possibly use him for any important task.

But God encouraged Moses by a great promise: "Certainly I will be with thee." Then Moses came to realize that God really was calling him and needed him. He accepted God's call and became one of the greatest men of all time as he gave his very life to do day by day just what God wanted done.

Although Moses was a famous man and few in all history have been so important or accomplished so much, it is true that every person has a place in God's plan and God needs every one of us. You see, the talents we have, our minds, our hands, our feet, were all given to us by our God and all of them are useful to him. In fact, what God wants done cannot be done until we are ready to do it for him.

Think how true this is. Years ago God needed someone to start the foreign missionary movement so he planned to send a boy named William. When William Carey was old enough he heard God's call and went out to India. God needed a great revival started and he decided to use a boy named Dwight. Dwight L. Moody did the thing God wanted done. God wanted his boys and girls to know about him and be taught Bible truths. He knew just the boy for that. His name was Robert, and Robert Raikes, as a young man, started the first Sunday school ever to be held in the world.

The same is true of important discoveries. It was Luther Burbank who helped God make luscious fruits and beautiful flowers by his experiments in botany. It was Thomas Edison whom God used to give his people more light. He whispered to Marie Curie the great secret of radium, and to a Negro, George Washington Carver, God gave the honor of performing miracles (we call them "synthetics") with peanuts and sweet potatoes.

I do not know exactly what God needs you to do but I do know he needs every boy and girl in the whole world. There are so many things to be done. There are diseases, like cancer and infantile paralysis, which can be cured when God finds the right person to help him. He needs boys and girls to help him take the atom and use it for good instead of evil. Then there are so many human problems God wants men to solve: the race problem, the war problem, the trouble between workingmen and employers, and a great many others. Somewhere there is a boy or a girl whom God is planning to ask to help him solve all of these problems and all the smaller problems too. There is enough to be done to keep everyone busy all their lives.

And God has a job for each of you right now. He wants you to study hard and work hard so you will have good trained minds and strong bodies and be ready to help him when he says to you one day: "I need you to help me build a better and happier world. Come, I will certainly be with you."

42

I Have a Daddy!

Now faith is assurance of things hoped for, a conviction of things not seen. —Heb. 11:1

Doris was a very little girl—just three years old—but pretty as pretty could be, with blond curls, sparkling blue eyes, and a big smile that made you want to smile back whenever you looked at her.

Now, though Doris was three years old, she had never in all her life seen her father. You see, he was a doctor and right at the beginning of the last war he had gone off to help take care of our servicemen on the islands of the Pacific, thousands of miles away. He was a very busy man and was so greatly needed that he had not had a chance to come home for a long, long time.

One day the minister from the church was calling in Doris' home and he had a nice long visit with Doris and her mother. Of course Doris knew the minister and greeted him at the door when he rang the bell. In fact, she almost opened the door before he rang the bell as she had seen him calling at other homes down the street and was sure he would stop there too. He always liked to call where there were boys and girls, and he used to say, (and I think he really meant it too), "Children are the most important people of all, you know."

The minister had scarcely been seated in the big chair by the fireplace when Doris said to him: "I have a daddy! And he is big and tall and has black curly hair and he's coming to see me sometime!"

Now of course the minister knew Doris had a daddy for he knew him very well indeed. In fact, it was Doris' daddy who came to the minister's house every day when he had influenza and was so very, very sick. He was the one too who sent a lemon around to the parsonage that Sunday afternoon when it became known all over town that the minister had lost his voice that morning in the pulpit and could not finish his sermon. Nothing serious was wrong except that the Rev. Frederick Brown had been cheering too hard at the basketball game Saturday night and his vocal cords were swollen. But people thought they had a good joke on the pastor as they said: "The doctor gave the preacher a lemon!"

Mr. Brown was thinking of these things, and Doris thought he had not heard her so she said again, a bit louder: "I have a daddy, and he's coming to see me someday!"

"Of course you have a daddy," said Mr. Brown, "and what a fine daddy he is, Doris."

Then he turned to Doris' mother and asked: "Is Walter coming home soon? He certainly has served his time and ought to have a chance to get back now, and I hope, be allowed to stay home."

"Yes," said the mother, "Walter is really on his way home and we expect to get a long-distance call from him any day now from San Francisco. You know, much as it means to me, it will mean even more to Doris for she has never seen her father. But oh, how she loves him, and how she asks me all kinds of questions about him, and when he will arrive. I can't begin to answer all the questions she asks."

So it was that a few days later, as Doris was looking out the window, she saw a tall man in uniform get out of a taxi right in front of the house. She was so excited she forgot to call her mother but opened the front door and ran down the walk. She looked up and saw a tall, big man, with curly black hair and a broad smile, and she pointed her little chubby finger at him and said: "You are my daddy, aren't you, now?"

The tall soldier stooped down and picked her up in his arms. He squeezed her tight and said: "Doris, my dear little girl, I certainly am your daddy, and I have been thinking of you and wanting to see you for so long a time it seems like an age! What a wonderful little girl you are—and you are my own Doris!"

Well, Doris and her mother and her daddy had a wonderful time that day and they sat and talked until it was very late that night and mother let Doris stay up too, for when a little girl's father, whom she has never seen comes home, you just forget what is day and what is night—and you don't care anyway!

When Doris did get so sleepy that mother thought it best for her to go to bed, she knelt down by her little cot and prayed a little child's prayer, but it was as fine a prayer as any grown man or woman ever prayed: "God, thank you heaps for bringing my daddy home to mother and me and please, God, let him stay with us—always!"

I don't know what you may think of Doris and her daddy and the way she waited for him and looked for him when she had never even seen him in all her life, but I'll tell you what the minister said in his sermon that next Sunday. He was talking about faith and he said: "I can explain what faith means by a little girl who is here this morning with her mother and her father. For three years she had never seen her father but her mother told her about him. Of course she believed in him, and she waited for him to come home and looked for him every day. That was faith."

Then he added some words that Doris did not understand. They were the words from the eleventh chapter of Hebrews which Mr. Brown used for his text: "Now faith is assurance of things hoped for, a conviction of things not seen."

43

You Can Do It!

I can do all things in him that strengtheneth me.
—Phil. 4:13

THE OTHER DAY, WHEN WALKING HOME AT LUNCH time, I passed a house with the doors and windows open to let in as much cool air as possible, for it was a very hot day, and I heard the voice of a boy cry out: "I can't do it!"

Now I do not usually look in people's windows or pry into other folks' affairs, but I did glance around hoping I might get a glimpse of that boy. I wondered if he had two legs, two arms, two eyes, and two ears. I knew he had a strong voice and good lung capacity. But I was curious to see just what kind of a cripple it was who thought he could not possibly do something which his mother had evidently asked him to do.

Then I began thinking of a friend of mine who has had every reason to say "I can't do it," but has refused to say those words, even though no one who sees him can understand how he can do any of the things he does. This man is a successful lawyer, and a member of the state committee which considers the program of help for crippled children, and he would never admit to you that he is in the slightest way handicapped, or that there is anything he could not do if he tried real hard. If I could introduce you to him, however, and you should put out your hand to greet him, you probably would be so surprised that you would forget to shake hands. In the first place, this man would be in a wheel chair. He has lost both his legs and one of his arms. Even his shoulder is gone on the left side. But I'll tell you what he has: A broad smile, a strong will, an unselfish spirit, and a heart full of love for his God and his fellow men. And he is busy doing good every day of the week.

Listen to his story. Joe Schnitzler has had sixteen operations. His trouble started when he was fourteen years of age. Although at that age he was a cripple, he worked his way through grade school and high school by tending furnaces and clerking in a store. Then this disease of the bone, which had been troubling him for quite a time, required an operation, and he lost his left arm. Later infection set in, which required another operation, and half of his shoulder on the left side was cut away.

In spite of his handicap, Joe Schnitzler determined to get a college education, and he enrolled at the University of Michigan. In the course of time the disease that had caused him to lose his arm began to affect his legs. Shortly afterward both of his legs had to be amputated to save his life. Even this tragic condition did not stop him. He kept on, finished his college course and received three degrees, the last one being his law degree.

This man in the wheel chair is more active than many of us who have two legs and two arms. He is in great demand as a lecturer. He has traveled all over the United States and Canada, and has toured Europe as well. He goes to ball games, and even goes hunting, and brings home the bacon too, or more accurately, the venison.

161

If you ask Joe Schnitzler the secret of his success, he will not hesitate to tell you that it is his faith in God. He says that at the time of one of his operations he really became discouraged, and felt that he wanted to die. He did not see how anyone could live and be of any good with his arms and his legs gone. But, as he tells it, the Lord spoke to him and said: "Joe, don't you worry. I will be with you all the time, and we will work it out together."

That is Joe Schnitzler's faith, and that is his life. Once he was offered $150 a month by a friend, and $100 by another. He was to receive the money as long as he lived. But Joe Schnitzler is not the kind of person to allow another to support him. He just thanked his friends and told them he was capable of taking care of himself, and he has proven that he is. He has formed the habit of always saying "I can, if I try," and never, "I can't."

If you will look in the fourth chapter of Philippians at the thirteenth verse, you will read the words of another unconquerable man: "I can do all things in him that strengtheneth me." The man who said that was being persecuted and was in a dark dungeon when he said it. He did not complain, however. He just did what he could. He talked to his guard about Christ, and won him to the Christian way of life. He had learned the secret of victorious living. No matter where he was or what his trouble, he said, "I can," and he did.

Are you ever guilty of saying "I can't"? If you ever start to say those words again, think of the man in the wheel chair who has no legs and only one arm but still says, "I can." Think of the man in prison who would not give up, but kept on preaching the gospel and winning people for Christ. Those of us who have our legs, our arms, our eyes, and our freedom, ought to thank God every day for his goodness to us. We should express our "Thank you" in terms of helpful services that make life happier for those who are not so fortunate as ourselves. So to that phrase "I can," add another to make it complete, and spark your muscles into action by saying: "I can and *I will!*"

44

The Girl Who Stopped the Streamliner

Be of good cheer.
—Matt. 9:2

MY UNCLE DAVE WAS A LOCOMOTIVE ENGINEER AND from him, when I was a boy, I heard many thrilling stories of the railroad. Many of these stories dealt with speeding trains sent on special missions. Some were about wrecks when the locomotive or coaches jumped the track and went hurtling down the mountainside. Others were stories of trains that carried presidential parties or candidates touring the country just before election. But some of the most interesting were the stories of the people the trainmen came to know by seeing them day after day as the train went speeding by their home or farm.

It was because of these stories that I took special pains to read in the newspapers the report of an incident that happened in Tennessee, where a little girl stopped a fast train, a streamliner running between Memphis and St. Louis. It was a fascinating story with a Cinderella touch to it, for the girl was poor, yet the fast train made a special stop right in front of her home and she was taken aboard and given one of the finest drawing rooms.

It seems that months before this, trainmen on the many trains that run on the Illinois Central tracks in Tennessee, began seeing a little girl sitting on the porch of her home, always waiting for them and always giving them a smile and a wave of her hand. She was so friendly and so faithfully waiting there when the trains passed that these men began to wonder who she was and why she was always ready to greet their train as it came down the track. So it was that one day conductor Johnny McNamara paid a visit to the girl's home to get acquainted. He found her name was Minnie Rose Webb, and she was a cripple, being paralyzed from the waist down. She was unable to walk or run and play, and spent the whole day sitting in a rocking chair on the front porch.

Now imagine how you might feel if you were unable to get around and had to sit in one place all day long. Perhaps Minnie Rose often felt discouraged or disappointed and blue. But somehow she managed to keep all such thoughts to herself, for instead of frowning or pouting or grumbling, she kept looking around for something interesting to see or someone to speak to, and whenever she saw someone she always smiled and sent a happy greeting his way. She got acquainted with the people who passed by her house, walking or driving, but the most interesting of all were the trainmen who operated the long freight trains and the beautiful, swift passenger streamliners.

It doesn't take a friendly person long to get acquainted, even at a distance, and so it happened that shortly after conductor McNamara met her and learned her name, all the trainmen who passed Minnie Rose's home came to know her by name and waved at her whenever they passed. They called her the mascot of the railroad line. They thought of her when they were home too, and talked with their wives about her, and what she might like or need, and then they would buy her presents and toss them off the train as they went by. But one present they kept thinking would be most useful of all, and so one day conductor McNamara's train stopped again in front of Minnie Rose's house, and what do you suppose the crew carried up to give her? A wheel chair to replace her rocking chair and enable her to move around the house from room to room as she wished. She was delighted with the chair, and thanked the men over and over, and smiled her sweetest smile. But even more interesting things were about to happen to Minnie Rose. The story of the cheerful little cripple girl who waved at the trainmen got into the newspapers and was told on the radio. The Shriners heard about it and they decided to give Minnie Rose a surprise too.

One night in March, the fast train—the streamliner from Memphis, and the best-equipped train on the line —stopped right in front of Minnie Rose's house, and she was carried onto the train and given a drawing room and the train sped off to St. Louis, where the Shriners have a fine hospital. There she was to be given treatment in the hope of curing her lameness. This must have been the happiest night of Minnie Rose's life, and I know she was deeply grateful and expressed her thanks to all who had any part in giving her this wonderful surprise.

I have never heard whether Minnie Rose made a speech or not, in the usual way speeches are made, by talking from a platform to a crowd of people, but I know her friendliness and her courage in suffering, and her cheerfulness in spite of her handicap, have been more eloquent than any words she might have spoken.

Jesus often said, "Be of good cheer." [1] He encouraged and helped people who were in trouble. He helped them to see the bright side and to have faith that life could be happy even if things were not just as they would like them to be. I believe Minnie Rose, by her smiles and her cheerfulness, is saying the same thing to hundreds of people, not only trainmen, but their friends and the people who read her story, people who have never seen or met this brave girl. Her very life says: "Be of good cheer. I know you can be happy for I have found how to be happy even though I must stay on my porch and be content to sit in a chair all day long."

So the little girl who stopped the streamliner, keeps on smiling and scattering happiness and good cheer farther than any of us can guess or even imagine.

[1] Matt. 9:2; 14:27; Mark 6:50; John 16:33.

45

Old Glory

Blessed is the nation whose
God is Jehovah. —Ps. 33:12

THURSDAY IS THE FOURTH OF JULY. THERE IS GOING to be a big celebration in town and people will be coming in from miles around. Seven high-school bands will play, besides the fife-and-drum corps from the American Legion, and the parade will be blocks and blocks long. I can close my eyes now and see the crowds all along Washington Avenue, with the boys and girls poking their heads out to see if the big procession has started down the street.

Yes, it will be a big day in our town and in our country and all around the world wherever Americans are found. American boys will be celebrating in France, in Germany, in the Philippines, in Japan, in China, in Iceland, in Alaska, and all around the globe. Wherever these Americans are they will be recognized by a banner waving in the breeze, that emblem of freedom, the American flag—"Old Glory."

Our flag is a symbol of the United States. We are able to see in it or read into it just what our country means to us: Its history, its ideals, its way of life, and its hopes for tomorrow. The very material out of which the flag is made is important. An American flag should always be made of bunting. A silk flag or a flag of any fancy material is not truly "Old Glory," for the material must represent the common man and suggest the sturdy, dependable, practical, "all-wool" character of the great majority of our citizenry. We do not glory in luxury and exclusiveness but we are proud of what we can have together and all can share. We are proud of the fact that every boy and girl who really tries and works hard has a good chance to achieve success and happiness in our great land of opportunity.

The making of our flag has meaning too. You cannot make a true American flag by taking a piece of white cloth and painting the red stripes and the blue field for the stars upon that white background. No, an American flag must be made of separate strips of red and white sewed alternately, a square of blue, and forty-eight white stars appliquéd on the blue field. You see, our thirteen original states stood together, not through force but because they wanted to be together. The forty-eight states that now make up our United States are all sovereign or self-governing states, but they stand united in a common purpose and loyalty. So it takes sixty-two separate pieces of bunting to make a genuine American flag that stands for independence and freedom as the great seal of the United States declares: *"E pluribus unum"*—one composed of many.

The colors are symbolic too. George Washington, in explaining the flag, once said: "We got the red from the mother country, but we have separated the red with strips of white showing that we are forever separated from England."

So white stands for liberty. It also stands for purity of purpose and for kindness. To see the white of our flag

169

reminds many a soldier and sailor of the Red Cross nurses with their white bandages ministering to wounded men on the fields of battle. It reminds us also of the ministry to suffering and starving people in times of disaster all around the world.

The red in our flag stands for courage, sacrifice, and suffering. It stands for the blood spilled on the battle-fields, where men have died protecting our freedom. It reminds us of the pioneers who sacrificed both property and life itself that our country might be carved out of the wilderness. It tells the story too of heroic men and women of science risking their lives in order that they might find cures for terrible diseases. It tells of mothers and fathers denying themselves for their boys and girls. Certainly it is crammed full of the glorious history of our heroes of yesterday and the sacrifices of courageous men and women of today.

Then there is the blue. We say, "true blue" and mean loyalty and dependability. That is what the blue of our flag means too—loyalty to the highest and best. Our national motto is suggested by that color: "In God we trust." Our Founding Fathers, whose trust was in the Almighty, wrote their faith into the very foundation of our national life. They knew the truth of that great text of the psalmist: "Blessed is the nation whose God is Jehovah."

Of course we'll be watching the parade next Thursday. We'll stand with bared heads as the flag passes by and be proud in our hearts of our native land. We will silently pledge anew our loyalty to be true to the noblest ideals for which "Old Glory" stands.

46

Pitch to Him!

*As ye would that men should do
to you, do ye also to them likewise.* ──Luke 6:31

It WAS THAT TWILIGHT GAME WHICH PROVED TO BE
Detroit's most popular game, with 39,957 fans in the
stadium. Wherever one looked there was a mass of people with all the colors of the rainbow in display. "Dizzy"
Trout was pitching for the Detroit Tigers and Joe Dobson began for the Boston Red Sox, though they played
five pitchers before the game ended. Everyone came ex-
pecting to see a great game and they did, for the final
score was five to five and the whole playing time was
filled with thrills. In the first inning the home team took
the lead with four runs to Boston's one, and the game
ended with three Detroit men on bases and a chance to
win with a big lead, but the Tigers failed to bring in
those final runs.

There was one bad bit of sportsmanship, however,
in the first inning, which lingered in the minds of the
fans. The Boston pitcher would not pitch to Hank
Greenberg, the big Detroit first baseman, who is famous
for his home run hitting. Two men were on bases and
one of Hank's mighty hits would bring them in. It was
also true that Greenberg began the game tying the record
of Boston's Ted Williams for the home run record in the
American League, each having sixteen home runs to his

credit for the season. (Incidentally, both Greenberg and Williams got a home run before the game was over, tying their batting scores at seventeen home runs each.) The Boston pitcher motioned to the catcher to step far to one side of the base and simply tossed him four balls, so far from the base that Greenberg would have had to take a step or two to reach them. We know this trick as a "pitch out." Of course the pitches were called "balls" by the umpire, and Hank had to walk to first base without having had a chance to swing at a ball. The crowd booed, as well they might. But the pitcher was not as smart as he thought he was, for the next man at bat was Pat Mullin, and he succeeded in batting out a home run which brought in three men along with himself, making a score of four to one.

Perhaps Joe Dobson, the Boston pitcher, thought in terms of strategy or playing to win the game, rather than in terms of giving an opponent a fair chance, but certainly his ball tossing looked like very poor sportsmanship to the spectators. Sportsmanship means not only playing fair and square, but giving the other fellow a fair chance to show what he can do. When a man is up at bat and the pitcher knows he is a dangerous man, it is a challenge to him to pitch the best ball he knows how in order to fool the batter. It is a test of skill between pitcher and batter. For the pitcher to throw the batter a poor ball, clear out of line of the base, is an admittance on the part of the pitcher that he is afraid of the batter, and since he cannot beat him in fair competition of skill; he will do it by taking advantage of a trick play.

The very purpose of our American games is to develop fine sportsmanship rather than to develop winners. It is much more important to be a good sport than it is to be a winner. If the winning is done by taking unsportsmanlike advantage of one's opponent, then even in the winning the winner has lost, for he has lost his own spirit of fair play and square dealing.

Jesus gave us the finest rule that could be thought of for any game, whether it is played in some sport or in the more serious business of living. It is called the Golden Rule and most of us know it by heart: "As ye would that men should do to you, do ye also to them likewise." In other words, treat other people just like you would like to be treated yourself.

How would you like to stand up at bat, knowing you can do a pretty good job of batting, and not be given a fair chance to swing at the ball? If you are the pitcher, remember how you would feel if you were the batter, and pitch the kind of ball that will give the other batter a fair chance to match his skill with yours.

This rule is just as important in the business of living too. Just now, for instance, there are thousands of people, including hundreds of boys and girls your own age, who are starving to death in Europe and in Asia just because they have not been given a fair chance to show what they can do. Their countries are in such a wretched condition there is not enough food to go around and the farmers do not have the seed and the farm tools and eqipment to plant and raise crops for tomorrow. The Golden Rule, and the spirit of true sportsmanship, says that we who have more than we need, should imagine what these starving people must feel like, and then share some of our food with them.

Can't you see how important the Golden Rule is? Whenever you see another fellow who is trying hard to do his best and yet doesn't have a fair chance, and you can give him that chance, as a good sportsman you will "pitch to him" and give him the opportunity he needs. You may not hear any cheers from the crowd, and you do not need any, but you will feel a deep satisfaction down in your heart and be happy that you had a little part in helping another get on his feet and stay in the game.

47

Radar

> *Give, and it shall be given*
> *unto you; good measure, pressed*
> *down, shaken together, run-*
> *ning over, shall they give into*
> *your bosom. For with what*
> *measure ye mete it shall be*
> *measured to you again.*
> —Luke 6:38

DURING THE LAST WAR THERE WAS A WORD THAT spelled magic whenever it was spoken. At first the word was a deep mystery, and few civilians knew what it meant. Later we began to hear some of the feats it could do. It was said that it could reach out in the dark or through the fog and spy out an enemy submarine and show where it was located. It could discover lost airmen floating on rafts in the great expanse of the ocean. It was part of the secret by which aviators could fly blind. It was called radar.

The other day a new story about radar was flashed on the front page of the newspapers. By the use of radar Signal Corps men sent out radio waves and touched the moon! It was said that these waves raced out so rapidly through space that they covered the 240,000 miles to the moon and the 240,000 miles back to the earth in just two and one half seconds! The experiments were made from a little shack on the coast of New Jersey near Asbury

Park. This was the same little shack where some of the most important and secret radar experiments were made during the war.

Another interesting fact about this moon visit by radar was that it was made in the morning instead of at night. We would naturally suppose that if you were going to shoot the moon it would be necessary to do it at night. But the two men who succeeded in reaching the moon by radar did it in the morning, just a few minutes before noon. Of course we know that at certain times of the month the moon is in the sky during the daytime. Often we can see it in the morning or the afternoon.

The imagination of newspapermen began to pop and crack when they heard about the moon experiment. They talked of space ships traveling to the moon and rocket planes visiting Mars to see if people lived there. Right in the news columns—not in the comic section, but on the front page—were stories that read like fairy tales. Radar had turned new pages of opportunity and opened undreamed of possibilities.

Since the end of the war many of our magazines have been printing pictures and descriptions that help us understand what radar is and how it works, but I suppose no one is able to understand it very well unless he knows a lot of mathematics and has studied a great deal of physics and has spent some time working with the sort of gadgets which are used in radar operations.

But the general principle of radar is said to be like the bouncing of a sound wave when it hits a big wall or a hillside, causing an echo to come back to the place where the sound was made. All of us are familiar with echoes. We yell "HELLO!" and then we hear in the distance what seems to be someone answering: "H-E-L-L-O-O-O-o-o!" If we call out, "WHO ARE YOU?" we do not get the answer to our question but the same question comes back: "WHO ARE YOU?" If we shout fast, the echo is fast; and if draw out our call, the echo comes back the same way.

I doubt if many of us will become radar operators or will spend a great deal of time with radar, but there is one kind of radar we are all using all the time. You see, the secret of radar is that as it sends out waves in all directions, these waves bounce back when they bump against any object in their way and then the returning waves are caught and recorded as to the distance they traveled and the direction they followed. All of us are sending out waves in all directions too—personality waves—and they work like radar. When they bump against someone else, they bounce back to us again.

Take a smile for instance. We radar a smile and it strikes someone and he smiles back. We sing a song and someone else starts humming it too. We say a kind word or do a kind deed and a good feeling bounces back to us. It is always that way, though sometimes we do not even know it is happening. Radar waves are invisible. Good-will waves are invisible too, at least most of them are, but our hearts record them when they bounce back and we feel that we have done just what we should have done.

Jesus gave us a radar text one day. At least it sounds to me like one. See what you think about it. He said: "Give, and it shall be given unto you." Doesn't that tell you how to get a good "bounce back"? Try it today— with everyone you meet!

48

A "Believe It or Not" Church

Upon this rock I will build my church; and the gates of Hades shall not prevail against it.
—Matt. 16:18

EVERYONE IS FAMILIAR WITH ROBERT RIPLEY'S DAILY "Believe It or Not" cartoons. I want to tell you the story of a "Believe It or Not" church. This church, believe it or not, has windows without glass. This church, believe it or not, was once used as a stable for mules. This church, believe it or not, was later converted into a headquarters for an army general. This church, believe it or not, was wrecked and rebuilt by the same army. This church is now, believe it or not, a signpost for all the directions of the compass.

This church is the Roberts Memorial Baptist Church at Bhamo, Burma. It was originally built by Kachin Christians and named for Dr. William Roberts, who was the first American Missionary to these Burmese people. The people loved their missionary friend so much they wanted their church building to be a memorial to him.

When the Japanese invaded Burma, Japanese soldiers took the town of Bhamo and then, to show their contempt for Christianty and the church, tore out the benches and other equipment of the Roberts Memorial Church and made it a stable for their mules. But such treatment did not discourage the members of the church.

They loved God and they loved their house of worship. They knew God understood their loyalty and so they just waited. Then the Japanese, seeing they had not caused the Christians to renounce their religion by simply desecrating their temple, drove out the mules, cleaned up the church building, and furnished it as the headquarters for their general.

But why would an army destroy or wreck a building and then get busy and build it again? You see, this was done by the American army, not the Japanese. The Japanese had fortified the church and so it was attacked by our troops. In these attacks it was battered and badly damaged. Then the American army, as you know, drove out the Japanese from Burma and took possession of the country. When they saw the damage they had done to the church, which had been a beautiful building and beloved by the Christians of the town, they were sorry and wanted to do something to make amends. They found there were a number of their men who had been stonemasons or carpenters or engineers before they joined the army, so they called for volunteers: "Who will help us rebuild the Bhamo church?" There was a fine response and the work was organized and started. Some who could not lay stone into the wall could gather the stone from the piles of debris and carry it to the masons. Others chipped off the old mortar and got the stones ready for the builders. Some carried sand and cement and mixed the mortar. Together they worked, and in a month's time they had the little church building almost as good as new.

Yes, I mentioned that this church had windows without glass. The windows had neither stained glass nor plain glass; there was no glass at all, just openings in the walls where the windows should be. This is not a curiosity in Burma, where most buildings do not have glass in the windows. The windows are for light and air, and since the climate is so warm there is no need of glass to keep out the cold and retain the heat of a stove. Of course mosquitoes, flies, and all kinds of flying bugs come in at the windows, but the people of Burma do not mind that for they are accustomed to these pests. They have the same kind of glassless windows in their own homes.

Those American soldiers were not satisfied when they finished the walls and roof of that church building. They knew there were many things needed which they could not make, such as benches, pulpit, organ, and all the other fixtures that are needed in every church. They might have said: "We are sorry we cannot make these things for you too," but they did not. They said: "Let us take up a camp collection," and they did. So these soldiers in the Bhamo area took up a money offering and sent a check for eleven hundred dollars—"For the further repair and beautification of the Roberts Memorial Baptist Church."

But what about the signpost? Well, just this: this church is so well known that when anyone traveling through Bhamo wants to know how to get to some other town or city in Burma, they are told: "Go to the Roberts Memorial Church, then turn east and go so many miles or blocks," as the case may be.

Every church should be a signpost, pointing men and women, boys and girls, to the road that leads to truth and righteousness. This "Believe It or Not" church in Bhamo has a great story to tell to the whole world.

49

A Bicycle and Two Prayers

*Whatsoever ye shall ask in my
name, that will I do.*
—John 14:13

SAM WANTED A BICYCLE. MOST OF THE OTHER BOYS
he knew owned bicycles, but he had never had one. He
could ride well enough for Bill and John, his chums, were
very generous with their bikes and often Sam would
take a ride. But he wanted a bike of his own.

Now Sam's mother was a widow and it was always
necessary to be very careful with their small allowance to
buy the things they needed: food, clothing, coal, and
other things about the house. Sam knew his mother could
not afford to buy a bicycle for him. Then he thought of
the minister's sermon about prayer the previous Sunday. The minister had quoted the words of Jesus: "Whatsoever ye shall ask in my name, that will I do."

"I know what I will do," said Sam, "I'll just ask for
a bicycle." It was a new idea to him and he was very
excited as he thought more and more about it. "I'll pray
tonight, and tomorrow my bicycle will be right on the
front porch waiting for me," he said to himself. So he
asked for a bicycle that night in his prayer, and he even
described the kind he wanted, and the color too. Then he
went to bed with high hopes but he could not get to
sleep for a long time because of the excitement over the
thought that tomorrow he would have a bicycle.

Sam was up early next morning and rushed to the front door to look on the porch. To his disappointment, no bicycle was there. Then he thought perhaps he had expected the bike to arrive too quickly. Of course it must come by express or delivery truck and would not come until later in the day. That must be the reason for its delay.

Then it was that Sam's mother saw disappointment written all over his face and she asked him what the trouble was. At first he said, "Aw, nothing, mom," but his mother knew Sam better than that, and soon he told her all about his desire and the prayer and how he had expected to find a bicycle awaiting him that very morning when he got out of bed.

Sam's mother had a long talk with him about prayer. "You see, Sam," she said, "you were using prayer as magic and that is wrong. God doesn't drop things out of the sky for us whenever we ask for them. He wants us to do our part and he will do his. Now first of all, remember Dr. Whitesall's sermon about prayer. He explained very carefully the meaning of 'in my name.' It means in harmony with, and in keeping with, Christ's plan to build his kingdom. A selfish prayer cannot be answered. Our prayer must be in the spirit of Christ. I wonder if God would want to help you get a bicycle if you want it just to ride around and enjoy for yourself. I think he would be interested in your having a bicycle only if by your having one you could be a better Christian, run more errands, and do more useful things for him."

Sam was very thoughtful. Yes, he remembered what Dr. Whitesall had said, now that his mother reminded him of it. God could not answer a selfish prayer, and his certainly had been a selfish one. He had thought only of the good times he could have riding his bike and the places he could go and, in fact, had even been thinking that if he got his bike he would not be able to help his mother as much as he had been doing for he would be so busy riding around.

"I'm sorry, mother," said Sam, "I guess my prayer was a very selfish one and I won't pray like that any more. Unless I can use my bike in helpful ways as well as to have fun just for myself, God wouldn't be interested, of course."

"Another thing," said his mother, "wouldn't it be better for you to ask God to help you find a job and help you stay strong and well so you can make money and save enough to buy what you really need?"

Sam was grateful to his mother and determined to be a better Christian by thinking of others instead of just himself, and by trying to learn how to pray in a way that God approves and can answer. He did get a job on Saturdays and many odd jobs shoveling snow that winter and mowing lawns the next summer. He was more thoughtful of his mother than he had ever been before. He helped her with the work around the house and brought her nice surprises he was able to buy because he was making money every week. He remembered the church too and the missionaries and always counted out a tenth of all he earned and called it "the Lord's money."

I almost forgot to tell you that Sam got his bicycle. It was really the neighborhood's bicycle, though, for Sam ran so many errands, for so many people, everyone called it "Sam's Service Special."

50

Beauty and the Beast

The wolf shall dwell with the lamb, and the leopard shall lie down with the kid; and the calf and the young lion and the fatling together; and a little child shall lead them.

—Isa. 11:6

THE FOUR-H SPEAKER WAS TALKING ABOUT CO-OPERATION, and he illustrated a point by telling of two cows he had seen as he drove along the road. He said they were standing side by side, facing in opposite directions, and each one, swinging her tail, was keeping the flies off the other's head. He called this "cow-operation!"

This reminded me of the fact that there are many examples of apparent co-operation in the animal world, and some of them are very peculiar indeed. There is the case of the rhinoceros bird, for instance. Not a large bird, he wears a gray-brown coat and a yellow vest. His bright red bill somewhat resembles a very red nose. He is tiny compared with his powerful armor-plated companion, the big rhinoceros. This animal is one of the most ferocious and dangerous of wild animals. However the bird is not afraid of him. In fact, bird and beast get along famously together. They form a sort of partnership. The bird lights on the rhinoceros' back and feeds on the ticks that crawl over it and irritate him.

We need not go to central Africa to see such a companionship. In our own country the cowbird is not an uncommon sight. He is a brownish-colored blackbird that often rides upon the backs of cows. The cows seem to enjoy their friendship.

The most unusual association of wild things I ever heard of is the reported custom of owls, prairie dogs, and rattlesnakes living together in the same burrow. The owls do often move in and occupy some of the extra rooms in the large underground homes of the prairie dogs but, of course, there is no love lost between owl and dog. The owls are really intruders and are not wanted, but impose upon the good nature of the little dogs and perhaps even prey on the little puppies when they get a chance. Owls feed on mice and other small animals, and I am sure they would not hesitate to feast upon a prairie puppy if he were handy. Now the rattlesnakes are even more unwelcome guests for they have no capacity for friendship unless it be inside their long slithery bodies! Undoubtedly they often crawl down the holes where prairie dogs live, but their visit bodes no good. They are most probably looking for food and there will be two or three little dogs missing when the snakes leave.

The most interesting case of co-operation in the animal and bird world which has come to my attention, is that of the crocodiles and the African plover or crocodile bird. Here is truly a case of "Beauty and the Beast." There is no uglier nor more brutally vicious reptile than a crocodile. On the other hand, the crocodile bird is a beautiful, frail, delicate bird. He could be crushed to bits by one flip of the crocodile's tail or even a slap of his tongue. Surprising as it may seem, however, the small bird jumps upon the crocodile's back and busily searches for insects. Then, if the crocodile's big mouth is open, he jumps right inside and industriously picks the crocodile's teeth!

This seems like a fairy tale, but naturalists who have studied the birds and have actually watched them enter the mouths of crocodiles, tell us it is really true. They say that sometimes the crocodile will even close his mouth when the bird is inside. That sounds like the end of the story for the crocodile bird, but it really is not because the crocodile does not want to injure the bird. He appreciates what his friend is doing for him—giving him free dental service by removing the leeches that cling to his gums and continually irritate his mouth. This provides food for the bird and gives relief to the crocodile. So the reptile opens his mouth and out hops the little bird without a feather harmed. Soon he is in another crocodile's mouth busy with his dental work.

Now crocodiles are fond of bird flesh and at every opportunity will eat a chicken or duck or crane, but strange as it may seem, they carefully protect the crocodile bird and he is as safe in their mouths as he would be high up on the limb of a tree.

Poets and prophets have found illustrations in bird and animal life, and one of the pictures of universal peace on earth suggests that when that wonderful time comes, "The wolf shall dwell with the lamb, and the leopard shall lie down with the kid; and the calf and the young lion and the fatling together; and a little child shall lead them."

51

Fists and Fingers

He took him aside from the multitude privately, and put his fingers into his ears.
—Mark 7:33

Today we are going to talk about something we all have—fingers. Although all of us have them, we probably do not realize how important they are, and how much they have meant to the human race. Just how many fingers do you have? Ten? Please hold up your hands and let me see, for I must be missing a finger or two myself. Will you count those fingers very carefully and tell me how many you find? Eight! That is the way I count too, and there is a real difference between a thumb and a finger. In a way there is a thumb for every finger on your hand, for the thumb will meet each one or all of them together. It is because of this fact that man has been able to do so many difficult things through the centuries and civilization has been able to advance. At least that is what scientists tell us. The thumb is one of the most valuable and useful things we possess, for it makes our hand an instrument of service in countless ways.

Just think what we can do with our hands because we have fingers and thumbs. Take the doctor or surgeon, for instance. He has trained, skillful fingers. I know a doctor who can take the two ends of a string, place them inside a penny matchbox, and tie those ends together with his fingers behind his back. He has practiced this difficult feat because in operations he does not wish to make long incisions, but incisions that are as small as possible, so they will heal quickly. With the small incision it is necessary to work in a very small space, but his skilled fingers can do it.

Think of the fingers of a great pianist or violinist. They are skilled fingers and have been trained by long years of patient practice. The jeweler's fingers must be skillful too, and the artist's fingers, and the typist's. Everyone's fingers are important and used constantly all day long.

Put a mitten on your right hand and see what a difference it makes. Of course if it is winter time and the weather is cold, you probably need a mitten, but think of the many things you could not do with mittens on your hands. Instead of the mitten, put on a boxing glove and that makes your hand even less useful and your fingers just do not count at all. Think of trying to trim a Christmas tree or playing the piano, or eating a big turkey dinner with boxing gloves on your hands!

I suppose none of us ever heard of anyone trying to do such things with boxing gloves, yet people do sometimes double their fingers up into fists—even boys and girls sometimes do such things. When fingers are doubled up into fists, the owner of those fists often causes trouble and usually gets into trouble himself. Noses are smashed, eyes are blackened, feelings are hurt, and enemies are made.

If we would just do a bit of thinking before using our fists, and remember how useless a fist is and how skillful fingers are, I think we would put away our fists and give our fingers a chance.

As we read about Jesus, we find that he was constantly using his hands and his fingers in helpful ways. One story tells of Jesus walking along by the sea of Galilee and there meeting a man who was deaf.[1] Because he was deaf, he also had difficulty in speaking, and would often stammer when he tried to talk. Jesus stopped and ministered to this man. He put his fingers into the man's ears and healed him of his deafness. He also touched his fingers to the man's mouth and healed his defect of speech. A beautiful story could be written about the hands of Jesus with those delicate, ministering fingers that brought blessings to all whom they touched.

A poet has written that Jesus has no hands today but our hands, and in a very real sense that is true. He inspires us to use our hands to do the things he wishes to have done. He depends upon our fingers to give the touch of kindness and the friendly service.

We must honor our hands, train them carefully, and use them well, that their work may always be pleasing to our Christ. Look at your hands again. Count those fingers again. Thank God you have eight fingers and two thumbs, and that you can use them for him. Then if ever you should find that hand of yours doubled up into a fist, making a club instead of an instrument of usefulness, open it as quickly as you possibly can and let those fingers loose to work for peace and friendship and love.

[1] Mark 7:31-35.

52

One Day at a Time

> *Be not therefore anxious for*
> *the morrow: for the morrow*
> *will be anxious for itself.*
> —Matt. 6:34

Do YOU EVER LOOK A JOB IN THE FACE AND THINK
it is too big for you? I mean an assignment at school, a
chore around the house, a terrible disappointment, or a
bad surprise that takes you off your feet and makes you
feel you just cannot take it? I'm sure all of us have times
when we feel that way.

I saw something the other day that may help you
handle anything that comes along, no matter how big it
may be. What I saw was two men painting a huge sign.
It was one of those signs so large that the men on their
ladders looked like spiders climbing around. The eye of
the face they were painting was as tall as the men themselves as they were seated on the scaffold. How in the
world could they paint something so much larger than
themselves and make it in proper proportion?

I found out the secret and I'll tell it to you. When
you learn the secret you can tackle a job of any size and
whittle it down to your own ability so you can handle
it. You may look as small as Jack the Giant Killer, but
you will be able to outsmart the giants just as he did if
you use the secret process.

Here is what I found. Sign painters work by scale.
When they are to paint a sign twenty feet high, they

make a sketch of their picture on a piece of paper or cardboard twenty inches high. Then they mark the small drawing off into one-inch squares. When they begin to paint the big signboard, they first mark it off into squares, but these squares are one-foot square instead of one-inch square. You see, by marking their work off in this way, they whittle the big thing down so it can easily be handled. With the signboard divided into squares, the painters just take one section at a time and that is not difficult for it is only one foot in size. Then they simply copy in that square what is on the one-inch square on their scale model.

In the Black Hills of South Dakota there is a giant monument called Rushmore Memorial. This is a mountain of rock out of which have been carved the likenesses of four of our national heroes: Presidents Washington, Jefferson, Lincoln, and Theodore Roosevelt. These figures are so tremendous in size that men working on them appear as flies. Gutzon Borglum, the sculptor who designed the memorial, used a unique method to whittle this job down to a size where he could handle it. He put the pictures of the men he wished to sculpture on stereopticon slides. Then at night he used the rock mountain as his screen and projected the huge pictures on the mountain. His men, hanging from long ropes, outlined the figures by tracing the pictures. Then they got busy with hammers and chisels, cutting into the great rock so that the faces stood out in relief.

Not only can big signs be painted and giant statues be carved by the scale method, but houses and great buildings can be drawn on paper to scale, and then the buildings constructed according to the measurements of the drawings. In fact, this is the way architects plan a building. They make drawings of each floor and each door, window, stairway, and so forth, using one half, one quarter, or one eighth of an inch to represent one foot in the actual building. In this way they can put the picture of a whole building on a piece of paper. This also makes it possible for them to whittle down the big job so they can handle it in small sections, and thus they can work out their problems right there on their drawing boards.

This secret of working to scale is not new, for men have been using the system for many hundreds of years. Draftsmen use it in designing all kinds of things: machines, tools, automobiles, trucks, locomotives, railroad cars—in fact, everything that needs to be planned before it is built, and that includes just about everything that men make.

Jesus gave the scale method secret to his disciples when he said to them: "Be not therefore anxious for the morrow: for the morrow will be anxious for itself." He was saying: Take one day at a time, whittle your job down, use the scale method, and divide your job into sections you can handle.

Nothing worth while can be done all at once. We must start and then keep doing one day's work at a time. And isn't it important that each day's work be the very best we can do, so that as it adds to the work of other days, it will all be of one good quality and all will stand up under any test that may come? Here is a good rule for fine work:

> Each day my best,
> Leaving to God the rest.